OUR COMMON FAITH

A Plea for Interfaith Harmony

DR. GHOULEM BERRAH

Introduction by Marguerite Berrah

Copyright © 2019 by Dr. Ghoulem Berrah Foundation

All rights reserved. No part of this publication may be reproduced, stored in a retrieval system, or transmitted in any form or by any means, electronic, mechanical, photocopying, recording, scanning, or otherwise, except as permitted under Section 107 or 108 of the 1976 International Copyright Act, without the prior written permission except in brief quotations embodied in critical articles and reviews.

Published by: Dr. Ghoulem Berrah Foundation
18851 NE 29th Avenue, Suite 700
Aventura, FL 33180 (USA)

ISBN: 978-1-7341201-0-3 (print)
ISBN: 978-1-7341201-1-0 (ebook)

Edited by Nana Yalley

Book Design by Deana Riddle

Photo Credit / Page: 30 "The beautiful minaret" – Cecil Images, Charles O. Cecil.

Printed in the United States of America

To Mubila

OUR COMMON FAITH
A Plea for Interfaith Harmony

with our warm wishes

Published by Dr. Berrah Foundation

on behalf of my beloved Husband

Contents

Homage to the Author   1

Introduction   5

Our Common Faith   19

Epilogue   95

Acknowledgments   105

Homage to the Author

by Nana Yalley

Dr. Ghoulem Berrah

To do justice to the life and accomplishments of His Excellency Dr. Ghoulem Berrah would take more than a few paragraphs of recollections from my memory. Certainly, his memoir, *A Dream for Peace*, and this book will do their part to deliver to the reader a portrait of a great man.

One anecdote that is worth mentioning was his persistence in reminding me of how much he loved his wife. It was a repetitive pattern that never ceased to amaze me. Each time we were together, he would interrupt our conversation as soon as his wife left his side, just to say how much he adored her. "You know, I wouldn't be who I am were it not for her," he would say. His opening statement was always the same as the accolades that followed, peppered with many praiseworthy tributes to his beloved wife. He would go on and on until she returned, and then he would immediately switch back to the conversation, as if to shield her from his affectionate poesy. He was always that way, and I came to cherish those moments. I looked forward to hearing his reaffirmation of genuine love—something so sacred. There was an elevated level of candid conviction that illuminated the persona of my dear friend and brother.

Never have I known an individual with so much compassion for his fellow brethren, always chasing a selfless drive to do what was best to achieve peace. When we met several years ago, it was at the boardwalk, on the water's edge, in South Florida. Our encounter, brief as it may have been, was borne out of Celestine Prophesy. Standing tall, with broad shoulders, exhibiting a fashionable and classy swag in a striped, fitted navy-blue suit, he smiled at me from afar as I approached, drenched in sweat, on my usual power-walk path. "Hello, my friend, how are you today?" he greeted with his signature smile. I stopped to take his outstretched hand. "I am doing well. Thank you for asking. How are you?" That was how it began. A friendship at first sight, which would by God's design to motivate him to finally decide to write his life's story. We were neighbors, but for the chance happenstance, our paths might never have crossed.

As time went by, we seemed to gel on many levels. I discovered a lot about the man and his boundless accomplishments. Our conversations were always deep and farsighted, at times spirited, yet very funny. I was hard-pressed not to pose the question, "When will you write your story?" His accounts of diplomatic rapprochement saw many gains in global political corridors, but there were also some painful losses that hit close to home. He spearheaded innovations that produced impactful outcomes in the world of biological science, and he recorded many selfless pilgrimages in strict harmony with his deep religious faith. I found him fascinating. He had chronicled a life that transcended the typical norm for high achievers, gone further than most humans in professional achievements and spiritual adeptness, yet those characteristics did not define his humble nature.

Throughout his life, he held firm to his honor in situations where it was severely tested. From him, I learned that the longer one struggles with something, the more we come to cherish it in the long run. His penchant to love deeply, and his disciplined engagement with his maker, were carved into his soul. Dr. Berrah faced the turmoil of political discourse head-on and challenged the status quo to embrace next practices. In the upper echelons of power, where he sat with diverse and cultured political leaders, he did his best work as a steward for peace, and from the grassroots, he empowered laymen to strive to reach their greatest potential.

When Dr. Berrah left the shores of his native Algeria as a young man to embark on studies in France, his heart was heavy, but his mind was set to return soon to help liberate his country from French colonial rule—by any means necessary. He had seen enough and lived a painful reality of subjugation, but he never accepted the policy of second-class citizenry. He refused to bow to any man or genuflect to any system of oppression.

His story, *A Dream for Peace*, is intricately woven in a delicately balanced oratorical sampling of episodes that chronicle a life's journey, seemingly hapless at times, yet with successful outcomes that serve as proof that his mission here on earth was ordained by a higher power. I continue to believe that greatness in a man or a nation is not by fluke. It is therefore necessary to harness the tenets of profound faith and constant prayer. Dr. Berrah had in him an endless fountain of living waters from which he drew an undaunted source of inner faith. Henceforth, his heartfelt involvement in the welfare of the average person did not distract him from the complex problems of the world at large. It is fair to say that all those who have met him have surrendered unconditionally to his sincerity, nobility, and witty personality.

With these few words, I salute my friend and brother, the traditional realist who did his very best work for Mideast peace, sewed the seeds of concord among people of different faiths, and served with distinction in his pursuit of Afro-Arab harmony. In so doing, he promoted the essence of dialogue for the ideals that are at their core, sustained by a sense of purpose. He was a true class act, an indisputable gentleman, who, out of his precepts of duty and honor, answered a greater call to serve in Africa and transmit to the world a diplomatic message for the greater good.

Introduction

by Marguerite Berrah

To introduce the author, His Excellency, Dr. Ghoulem Berrah, who happens to be my beloved husband, is not too challenging an endeavor because he was an atypical character gifted with an incredible amount of talents and blessed by a unique destiny.

He was born on May 29, 1938, in Aïn Beïda, a small town at the foot of the Aurès Mountains, in northeastern Algeria, into a humble and very proud family that had descended from Arabized Berbers, famous for their tenacious determination, bravery, and acute sense of honor. In those days the country was considered a part of mainland France.

His father, Hamadi Berrah, was a local jeweler who passed away when Ghoulem was only five years old. Nonetheless, surrounded by the family's clan and his father's twelve brothers, his mother, Lalla Zebida, a young and very pious woman, took good care of the education of her son and three daughters.

He was pampered by his mom but she instilled in him a strong discipline at an early age. She would wake him up at five o'clock in the morning, the exact time when the elders awoke for their morning prayers, and walk him through his morning ritual until he was ready for Qur'anic school about two blocks away from their home. He would return at seven o'clock, eat breakfast, and head to kindergarten.

She wanted to ensure his thorough comprehension of the Qur'an and Islam. She also instilled in him a respect and understanding for other faiths. Her two best friends were of the Jewish faith. As a child she would usually ask that he go to the house of her friends every Sabbath to turn on the lights for them. The precepts of their religion forbade them from engaging in certain mechanized activities.

Witnessing the behavior of the French colonists, Ghoulem was a very alert young boy and would react promptly each time he faced a situation he thought was wrong and would challenge the person right away. The fight for justice was engraved in his DNA.

The first incident happened when he was ten years old. His school's heating system was a wood-burning cast furnace. Due to the overwhelming levels of smoke that flowed into the classroom whenever fresh firewood was placed in the unit, no student was permitted to put logs in it during recess.

On one extremely cold day, one of his French classmates tossed a log into the stove right before the end of recess. When the math teacher, a Frenchman, entered the classroom and saw the gradual release of black smoke, he immediately turned to Ghoulem and yelled: "This is an Arab deed!" Without hesitating Ghoulem replied, "No, sir, this is a French deed." Obviously irritated, the teacher stared him in the eyes and posed the question directly, "So who is responsible for the faux pas?" "I do not know. Let the culprit come forward," he replied with a child's insolence.

The teacher had singled him out because he was the only Algerian in class that day. His audacity was considered an act of disobedience meriting a three-day suspension. It was his first revulsion against racism and colonialism. Whenever he recounted the story, he recalled the mean behavior of his teacher, and the effect was a surge of his anticolonialist sentiment and instincts. He decided he would never accept injustice.

The second incident occurred when he was fourteen. He worked hard to achieve high academic scores. At the graduation ceremony he received almost every award, including one for excellence and the prestigious City of Batna Award. A separate city award was given to the top girl in her class. The students stood in line waiting to go to the podium. He was second in line behind a French girl. The racist colonial mayor of the city presided over the award ceremony. When the girl walked up to receive her prize, he planted a kiss on her cheek, congratulated her, and handed over the prize.

She walked off beaming with pride.

Ghoulem moved into the position and reached for a handshake, but instead, the mayor shoved the award in his hand to avoid making skin contact and quickly turned to look at the students behind him. Without hesitation he staged an immediate anticolonial protest on the spot and dropped the large, beautiful, engraved hardcover book. It crash-landed with a thud on the ornate table and the audience gasped. He stared into the eyes of his bewildered classmates and ambled off to his seat.

No wonder after finishing high school, as a medical student in Bordeaux, France, he became an activist for the independence of Algeria and all French colonies. When the Algerian War burst out, his activism reached a peak. He was pursued by the French police, who were ready to serve him an arrest warrant. He chose to sacrifice his life for his country, and made the decision to flee from France and join the Maquis Guerrilla Fight.

Ghoulem trekked across the Pyrénées mountain range, crawling on his knees and elbows to avoid detection, until he got to the Spanish border town of Pamplona.

He was arrested by the Spanish Guardia Civil, put in jail, and released after three months as part of a prisoner swap. He was then able to cross the Mediterranean and join the fight.

He was stationed in the northern part of Morocco at the border of Algeria. With his companions he conducted covert operations into Algeria to deliver weapons and ammunitions until the French army made matters worse by placing barbed wire and land mines on the grounds to prevent border penetration.

He moved to another position in a training camp where he was in charge of providing fighters with medical assistance. He extended his assistance to Moroccan villagers and was asked by Moroccan authorities to work in different facilities.

One of the facilities was located next to Rabat, the capital city. He took the opportunity to organize the Algerian students who also fled from France to settle in Morocco. Because of the unmatched Moroccan hospitality, he was introduced to several ambassadors and managed to secure some scholarships for Algerian students.

He was in contact with different student organizations around the world. As the result of his activities, he was invited to tour Eastern Europe and went to the People's Republic of China to represent the youth of the third world and the FLN (the Algerian Revolution Organization). He had the opportunity to meet face to face with Chairman Mao Zedong , the leader of the People's Republic of China, when he was only in his twenties. He visited local universities to conduct lectures on the Algerian Revolution.

When he departed from China shortly after setting foot in Rabat, he was summoned by Dr. Francis Hammond, the director of Cultural Affairs for the US Embassy, with whom he had been in contact for some time.

During their meeting, he informed him about the ten Fulbright Scholarships that the US government had offered to Moroccan students that were not attributed. He wanted to redirect the awards to the Algerian students with the blessing of the Moroccan government. With the assistance of Princess Lalla Aicha, King Mohammed V's daughter, an avid supporter of the Algerian cause, to whom he was introduced by his dear friends the Hassars, the scholarships were awarded to the Algerian students, himself included.

It was a fateful occurrence, an unexpected opportunity to make people of the United States, such a big power, get acquainted with the Algerian suffering.

At the time, President Eisenhower wrote to the king of Morocco: "The United States government fervently hopes for an early end to this war and to all the suffering and danger which it entails." Eisenhower would combat potential communist advancement around the globe. He was engaged in discussion with the President of France, Charles de Gaulle, to apply the principle of self-determination to Algeria.

Upon landing in New York, volunteers from the Institute of International Education (IIE) working with the State Department saw to the Algerian students' safety, security, and comfort.

Ghoulem was enrolled in a three-month program at Bennington College in Vermont offering intensive English studies. At the end of the course, he received an invitation by the US Senate Foreign Relations Committee to give a presentation in Washington, DC. During his meeting with the senators, he clarified the fact that the FLN was not a communist organization. His trips behind the iron curtain were motivated by the needs of the revolution.

After completing successfully his assessment test, he was enrolled in the department of Microbiology at Indiana University's College of Arts and Sciences.

While studying to reach higher achievements, he began targeting churches, temples, colleges, and universities across the Hoosier State for speaking engagements. As the word got around, he received invitations to speak in other forums and did his best to shine some light on the dark trenches of colonial tyranny.

With his vigorous activism, slowly but surely various liberation movements began to sprout out of the grassroots in support of the Algerian cause. Congressional representatives received petitions from constituents imploring them to push for a cessation of the war.

His tireless efforts had awakened the consciousness of many who until then had not been familiar with the Algerian struggle. It wasn't long before the message resonated and snowballed beyond imagination.

Barely two years after being at the university while pursuing his master's degree, he achieved a major scientific breakthrough regarding the selective inhibition of DNA. His discovery was published by major scientific magazines, *The Journal of Bacteriology*, and *Biochemical and Biophysical Research Communication*. He was listed in American Men of Science (a biographical reference on leading scientists) and was elected a member of Sigma Xi, a society honoring scientific achievement. A few years later it became a member of the New York Academy of Sciences.

As he endeavored to complete his PhD, because of his discovery, he began receiving teaching offers from many prestigious universities proposing that he join them after the completion of his doctorate. He chose the University of Yale School of Medicine.

Introduction

During his college years at IU, Ghoulem visited the United Nations as often as possible to keep a close eye on political developments in Algeria. He was frequently the guest of Côte d'Ivoire's representative to the UN, Usher Assouan, who was an old friend of his from his years in Bordeaux.

A meeting of fate occurred in May 1962 when President Kennedy's diplomatic guest Félix Houphouët-Boigny, the president of Côte d'Ivoire, asked Ghoulem through his friend Usher to meet with him in New York.

The encounter, held at the Waldorf Astoria Hotel, was very warm. President Houphouët-Boigny asked him to come to Côte d'Ivoire and help develop the country. Although touched by the offer, he expressed his wish to return to Algeria.

Soon after his beloved country became independent, he flew to Algeria with the desire to serve his country. He was disappointed beyond belief. He had hoped that after such a harsh war Algerian leaders would seize the opportunity and the high road for an immediate peace and justice for all who chose to stay and help the new nation rebuild itself and become a strong democracy.

Instead, there was a mass exodus of French immigrants because they were given a stark choice between the suitcase or the coffin, so they chose the suitcase. The new president with whom he had a meeting failed to take any action to stop the practice amid the rampant chaos in Algiers.

Upon discovering that the president had opted for an orientation toward a bold form of socialism and surrounded himself with Trotskyists, Ghoulem was overwhelmed by sadness and decided to return to the United States after only ten days.

He completed his PhD and was enrolled as a lecturer at the Yale School of Medicine. Although he was content to be a lecturer in such a prestigious university and enjoyed the interactions with his students, he secretly had an overwhelming feeling that something was amiss, and his life's purpose was not being fulfilled. There was no doubt in his mind that his life's mission was somewhere else waiting patiently for him.

As he recounted to me, slowly but surely his dreams morphed into voices that echoed louder on his conscience.

Considering the excruciating pain and suffering inflicted on his people in the aftermath of the Algerian war, a bloody war that had left in its wake countless numbers of martyrs, he felt a burning desire to engage. He made the determination to work for a better world and find an alternative to war. Ghoulem decided to dedicate his life to public service and work to establish a better understanding among all people through dialogue, for the sake of peace and justice.

Two years after starting his tenure at Yale, he resigned in order to go and participate in Africa's development and work to achieve peace around the world. He contacted the president of Côte d'Ivoire through his ambassador to notify him that he was ready to accept his offer. The ambassador called to inform him that the Ivorian leader looked forward to his arrival.

Félix Houphouët-Boigny, the first president of Côte d'Ivoire after the country gained independence from France, known as the Sage of Africa, was a moderate and extremely wise leader who championed dialogue as the only effective means for resolving any conflict between humans or nations. This was a belief that Dr. Ghoulem Berrah totally espoused. He dropped a high-profile scientific career to embrace diplomacy. As special advisor to the president, ambassador and emissary, he was an untiring artisan for peace.

His pragmatism and humility led him to favor behind-the-scenes diplomacy as most effective. In doing so, he deployed an exceptional talent. He started by bringing peaceful relations between Côte d'Ivoire and Algeria.

As an ambassador for peace, he challenged himself to dedicate all his energy and diplomatic resources to help solve the Israeli-Palestinian crisis. He knew there was a taboo associated for an Arab being seen as cozying up to an Israeli. He was risking his life every single day, yet he continued to be determined without holding back any efforts.

In 1976, with a group of people, he was able to initiate the first secret meeting in Paris between the ICIPP (Israeli Council for Israeli-Palestinian Peace) and the PLO of Chairman Arafat.

He also helped secure dialogue between the French government and Somalia regarding the independence of Djibouti. In addition, he helped transfer the port of Berbera to the United States, and much more.

A devout Muslim, cooperation and respect amongst people of all faiths was a major concern to him. He deployed a lot of efforts to develop personal relationships with Christians, Jewish, and Buddhists for the sake of peace and fraternal harmony.

My Story

How do I came into the picture?

I was born in Grand Bassam on the seashore of Côte d'Ivoire, on the west coast of Africa, into a privileged family. My dad, Gabriel Ollo, was a pharmacist, and my mom, Suzanne Ollo, was a schoolteacher. They both worked for the Central French Colonial Administration for West Africa, whose headquarters were in Dakar, Senegal. The first-born child, I spent my childhood in Dakar with three of my siblings. We were spoiled by our parents who thought that nothing was good enough for their children.

Like my husband, I was raised in a very religious family. My parents were Roman Catholic and walked their children through the Catholic faith, baptism, catechism, first communion, and confirmation. We would attend mass every Sunday. Mom was a very pious person. At an early age, she would have us participate in the rite of penance in observance of Good Friday's fast by having us eat only a piece of bread dipped in a cup of sugared water. The whole day was spent in a mourning atmosphere in remembrance of Jesus' Trial. The atmospheric perfume of sadness left an imprint on me all my life long on Good Friday.

Mom had also a special devotion to the Virgin Mary that she communicated to me. She would pray the Rosary and teach us the importance of prayer in our lives and watched over our daily prayers.

Due to the importance of Islam in Senegal, we were surrounded by Muslim families. We would watch as they walked through their ritual, observe the month of Ramadan fasting, and would participate in Eid, the end of the Ramadan celebration. Our neighbors would bring some homemade sweets to us (sweets being a symbol of happiness). We would also go and congratulate them.

When I turned ten, I ended primary school and was sent to a boarding school in France for a better academic education. With no surprise I was enrolled in a Catholic school, one of the best schools in France for girls, Sainte Marie de Neuilly, in an upscale neighborhood at the doors of Paris. The school, run by the Sisters of Saint François Xavier Community, was usually ranked number one because of their hundred percent rate of success at the baccalaureate (end of high school exam).

By their practical approach to religious education, they helped strengthen my love of God and my love of my neighbor. On our day off, each of my classmates and I were assigned to assist, on a weekly basis, a girl from a difficult neighborhood. We would spend the afternoon with her, discuss her problems, and bring her some support before she was taken home. We would pay frequent visits to elderly people without a family, organize a special Christmas party for handicapped children, and more.

The Sisters' mission was to teach, to raise, and to evangelize, and their goal was to link together culture and faith, humanity and spirituality, audacity and commitment. Through education, they wanted to make sure that each student become independent, responsible for her own deep choice and commit herself to make others feel God's presence in the world by surrounding them with love.

On the eve of Côte d'Ivoire independence from France, my parents moved back to their beloved country. My dad established his own pharmacy, decided to get into real state as a developer, and became a successful businessman. My mom dedicated herself to teaching in public schools.

Upon finishing high school, I started studying pharmacy at the Paris Faculty of Pharmacy. Due to the May 1968 turmoil in France, especially in Paris, the town was paralyzed; there were no classes and no exams. The school year was lost. My parents sent me to Lausanne, Switzerland, to pursue my pharmacy studies. Switzerland should be a more stable country, they thought.

The hand of the Lord was upon me. He took me to Switzerland, where I met my beloved husband.

When we met, I was at the University of Lausanne and he was already a diplomat. It happened at the residence of the Côte d'Ivoire ambassador and representative to the United Nations Office in Geneva, a relative of mine.

We were the perfect match because he and I found a lot of topics of mutual interest. I could pick his brain on biology, and my biology professor was impressed by my exponential progress in the field. History was my favorite topic, and his work as an ambassador for peace was in synchronicity with what I had been taught and had embraced, that anyone in the world is my neighbor. I was always ready to accept any sacrifice to help him reach his goal for peace.

When I graduated from the school of pharmacy, I enrolled at the Graduate School of International Studies in Geneva to be completely on the same page as him. We lived in Côte d'Ivoire while he was touring the world in his quest for peace and moved to the United States later when he retired from politics.

I had never met such an enthusiastic human being. A witty personality, my Love was always ready to put a humorous note here and there, even in a difficult situation to try to soothe the atmosphere. He loved to sing in private. When we drove for a long distance, such as from Denver, Colorado to Gaspard, Wyoming, we didn't need to play any CDs because he would entertain us with his melodious voice, singing in English, Arabic, or French.

Generous beyond belief, he was Santa Claus to everyone, trying to cater to others' needs. He carried a tiny book of quotes and would emphasize that every single person needs something different. "Happiness is a peanut if someone is in need of a peanut." "Happiness is a blanket if someone is in need of a blanket." He cared for each person he met. He would provide anyone with spiritual, material, or intellectual assistance, and take time to listen to them. As a consequence of his selfless nature, others would always come first.

All these qualities made him a very dedicated and exceptionally loving husband. In this ideal picture, in our ordinary life I would beg to disagree with him in only one point; he wanted everything to be done quickly without wasting a second, but in most circumstances I preferred to take some time. In stark contrast, in his work as an ambassador for peace, he was determined to cultivate an angelic patience and perseverance.

The fact that he was a man of faith was most important to me. He was a devout Muslim happy to be married to a Roman Catholic woman who took her faith seriously.

Note to Readers

Our Common Faith is an abstract of a larger book titled *A Dream for Peace: An Ambassador's Memoir*. In *Our Common Faith*, the author put in perspective his own faith and his commitment towards other faiths. Step by step, he walks the reader through interfaith harmony and a plea for peace.

He wanted the fundaments of his thinking to be materialized into a foundation that carries his dream for interfaith harmony and peace. If you wish to know more, please visit his foundation's website, www.berrahfoundation.org.

Our Common Faith

Religion has always been my ultimate sanctuary. I practiced my faith with an innate and inescapable awareness that I also needed to take a stand on some things, albeit in a discreet way. My convictions and beliefs are essential to my sense of purpose and loyalty to the Almighty. Endowed with these principles, my commitment extended beyond the personal to the needs of the faithful who sought to pray in a safe haven.

I finally decided to embark on a long-awaited trip to the village of Satama-Sokoura—the hometown of my faithful chauffeur, Toureé Mama, to meet his family for the first time. We drove for hours to the central part of Côte d'Ivoire. On the outskirts of town, he turned on a small street and passed by a nineteenth-century mosque, distinctively situated a few yards from the main road. Out of sheer curiosity, I asked him to pull over. I inched closer to the property and touched the retaining wall. The cascading sun-dried bricks were molded from mud and clay, and hand-plastered by workers typical of an epoch of bygone times. Massive blocks of sandstone had been used to reinforce the main entrance, and support beams had been nailed together to hold up the outer and inner perimeter walls. In keeping with tradition from the period, red clay was used for surfacing on the outside, around the windows, and inside the arches of the doorway. I was fascinated by the historical significance of the monumental structure, which was seemingly in danger of falling apart. "I have to do something about this," I said. "The mosque must be saved from further structural damage." Touré agreed.

Within weeks, my architectural team provided details on the scope of conservation work needed to preserve the structure's relics. After lengthy discussions, I put forth a plan to restore and expand the space. I wanted to modernize without compromising its original features, but most importantly, I wanted to ensure that it would be developed to accommodate the growing community. I counted on the local workforce of mostly self-taught masons and apprentices to take up the task, and I wasn't disappointed. Everyone was disciplined and reliable. We completed the project on time, to the delight of the community's faithful Muslims.

The Adjamé mosque, located in a very popular and crowded neighborhood, can be seen towering over the open marketplace, especially in the evening, when the waning sun begins to set, casting a blissful ray of light across Abidjan. It stands tall in the northern part of the city's impoverished neighborhood. In the past, the massive building presented a fading, corroding structure that seemed more like a concrete façade, bridging an outward appearance to conceal a less-pleasant reality. The wear and tear had been due to neglect and insufficient maintenance over the years, worsened by adverse effects of seasonal rains and other climatically hazardous factors. Having successfully completed the Satama-Sokoura project, I was motivated to take on another reconstruction project to improve the neighborhood.

When I first set foot on the property, the pillars and columns reminded me of the mosque in the holy Islamic city of Medina. Although the frames of the building were well preserved, the structure required substantial conservation work in addition to a paint job, flooring, and installation of new facilities. A team of experts assured me that they could restore the fading ceiling to its original appearance. This was a key factor in my decision to award the contract.

To get the project underway, I raised the much-needed funds and provided additional financial infusion of my own. I hired the most skillful construction workers in the city and set out to micromanage the process like a seasoned project manager, without fully appreciating the daunting demands it was about to place on my schedule. New flooring was the first to be installed by my team, but the rebuilding of amenities was outsourced and the final painting touch-ups were completed at the end of the project. President Houphouët-Boigny was one of the financial backers. His generosity and support was unmatched. He was eternally committed to the success of such projects, regardless of their religious orientation, but especially, in the case of Islam—the religion of the poor. I knew I could always count on him.

As a passionate devotee, the president took his faith very seriously. He had the great misfortune of watching his mother die in his arms. "In her final moments, I conjured up enough courage to baptize and give her the name Marie," he confided. "That was quite an extraordinary act of faith, Mr. President," I said. "I can't even begin to imagine how difficult the experience must have been." After years of attending mass with his wife in the neighborhood parish, he decided to transform an office in his private residence into a chapel. From then on, he celebrated mass at home with the local Apostolic nuncio.

At the time, Archbishop Justo Mullor Garcia, the papal nuncio and advisor to His Holiness Pope John Paul II, had been in Côte d'Ivoire for several years and developed a very deep friendship with the president. He had become his personal confidant and was more than happy to officiate mass at the chapel. The standing invitation to join in prayer sessions was a privilege for my wife and me, and we looked forward to hearing Monsignor Mullor's powerful sermons, imbued with deep interpretations of biblical passages.

On a few occasions, the mild-mannered and polite Secretary of the Nunciature, Monsignor Timothy Broglio, was the substitute celebrant, ever so graceful and spiritually adept. As a practitioner of Islam, and one who is well versed in the teachings of the Holy Qur'an, I recognized the similarities between both religions.

The relationship between President Houphouët and Monsignor Mullor evolved into the space of confessor and spiritual counsel. However, Monsignor Timothy Broglio moved away after years of service in Côte d'Ivoire and took on another assignment at the Vatican, where he quickly rose through the ranks until Pope Benedict appointed him archbishop for the US military.

With Monsignor Mullor and the president.

My wife and I arrived at the official residence on a beautiful Saturday afternoon to join the president for mass. When he walked into the living room, he seemed a bit bothered. He had been speaking privately with an individual who pressed him for a favor and rubbed him the wrong way. "I am very disappointed at the irrational context of the conversation," he expressed quietly to me as we walked into the chapel. Once seated, we were directed to the Gospel according to Luke, chapter 6, verses 29b, 30, and 31, the liturgy of the day. The topic was about responding to solicitations:

"And from him who takes away your cloak, do not withhold your tunic either. Give to everyone who asks of you. And from him who takes away your goods do not ask them back. And just as you want men to do to you, you also do to them likewise."

These words took on a deeper meaning for the president. As far as he was concerned, what he heard in the Gospel amounted to a divine call for immediate action. He came up to me after mass and asked that I summon the individual to his residence. It was then that I realized the profound impact of the Gospel's effect on his judgment. I was deeply touched. The gentleman was beyond grateful to be at the receiving end of the president's generosity.

The clergy had set aside a large plot of land for a future cathedral building in Plateau's business district right in the heart of Abidjan. The spectacular city views provided a backdrop for what was expected to become a masterful architectural work of art. Planning for the project had gone on for months with the involvement of many faithful Catholics in the community, but we encountered difficulties in our attempts to secure adequate financing. When the president stepped in and made a large contribution to break ground on the construction, Aldo Spirito, a highly respected Italian architect, was hand-picked to design the cathedral. His final model was a mockup of the towering figure of Saint Paul.

Monsignor Mullor rolled up his sleeves and got down to work like a master foreman. He was very engaged in the many phases of construction, maintaining a shrewd vigilance and exceptional tenacity to ensure a perfect outcome. As the designated interior designer for the cathedral, he oversaw décor, selecting a number of beautiful stained-glass tableaux that pulled in a cast of colorful rays from the sun. Archbishop of Notre Dame d'Afrique Basilica in Algiers donated the church bells. Monsignor Mullor was hands-on until the very end.

Saint Paul's Cathedral.

He arranged the second visit to Côte d'Ivoire by His Holiness Pope John Paul II for the consecration on August 8, 1985. The neighborhood echoed with sounds of heavenly bells that announced the commencement of the magnificent ceremony.

I was in attendance with my wife, who had been selected by Monsignor Mullor to join the lucky few to receive the Holy Communion from the pope. Within minutes after the ceremony's conclusion, Monsignor Mullor and the pontiff boarded a helicopter to the airport for a chartered flight to Cameroon.

Circling over the city of Abidjan, His Holiness praised the grandeur of President Houphouët-Boigny during an especially candid moment: *"It would suffice one more head of state such as the one I met in Côte d'Ivoire to change Africa and perhaps the world."* Monsignor Mullor, who had become a dear friend of ours, shared the extraordinary moment with my wife and me.

President Houphouët with Pope John Paul II.

Murmurs from the country's majority Muslim population grew louder by the day, mostly due to the much-acclaimed publicity regarding the scope of the president's involvement in a "Christian project." Some complaints of a lack of fairness in needed investment distribution across the two major religions were duly noted, but such sentiments were not expressed openly. It had long been clear to me that the city of Abidjan, with its modern infrastructure, was in dire need of a new mosque. There was an open tent with aluminum roofing in the exclusive Cocody neighborhood of Riviera Golf, where my fellow Muslims and I congregated for Friday prayers. We had been subjected to many a difficult situation, particularly during the monsoon season rains.

The stacks of aluminum sheeting on the roof of our prayer shelter were not exactly soundproof, and the clatter of the heavy tropical rains rattling off to deafening levels made it impossible to hear the Imam's sermon (*khutbah*). As I prayed, I imagined being in a tranquil space, insulated from all distractions, and I continued to reflect on a viable solution to end the torment. I prayed to Allah to show me the way. At the completion of prayers on a stormy Friday afternoon, I took to the floor and announced to everyone, "The president will build a mosque for us." The statement came out of my mouth, and I meant every word with all my heart. The only problem was, I had not discussed the matter with the president. The congregation responded with much elation and a collective sigh of relief. Some applauded and chanted *"Allahu Akbar"*—praise the Lord.

I went from there to have lunch with the president at the residence. His close confidant, Abdoulaye Diallo, who had been at the mosque that afternoon, had arrived earlier to thank the president for his "selfless commitment." President Houphouët was surprised, but he played along until I got there. During lunch with two of his ministers and me, he suddenly looked at me and smiled. "So, I heard that Dr. Berrah has taken it upon himself to enlist my commitment for a new mosque in the Riviera?" I laughed and nodded approvingly. However, the minister of state, a Protestant, did not attempt to hide his displeasure. The president deflected his concerns and continued the conversation.

It wasn't very long before he quietly threw his support behind the project. I secured a large plot of land only a few yards away from the old mosque. The final blueprints included an adjacent complex to house a conference room with two or three lecture halls and a large parking lot. The local mayor, who was not very pleased with the idea of a mosque in the neighborhood, carved out a piece of the plot and set it aside for a "future project." His underhanded actions, which were revealed long after construction had begun, angered many of the youth in the Muslim community.

We halted the bidding when renowned architect Pierre Fakhoury, a Lebanese Christian and a Prix de Rome recipient, donated the blueprints of a model inspired by the beautiful Obhur Mosque in a suburb of Jeddah, Saudi Arabia. I wasn't familiar with that particular mosque, even though I had visited the city several times before. The task ahead was more difficult than I had anticipated. After weeks of pursuing leads, I learned of a major breakthrough from the president when I paid him a visit following the completion of Friday prayers. "The family of Bintou wishes to donate proceeds from the sale of her estate to help finance the project," he told me. I was pleasantly surprised and elated to hear the great news. He was referring to a very dear friend, Mrs. Bintou Camara from among the Muslim community, who had been called by the Almighty not so long ago. It was the will of Allah that had worked such a miracle, and I was certain that she was smiling upon us. The president himself made a large contribution and decided to convene a meeting with leaders of the Muslim community, Pierre Fakhoury and the director of the Grands Travaux,[1] Mr. Antoine Cesareo.

Attendees to the town hall included the head of the Economic and Social Council (the third most influential person in the country), young Muslim organizers, and prominent officials from affluent Muslim circles. President Houphouët presented the project to the audience and introduced Pierre Fakhoury, who unveiled the model and described the structure in detail. "Can you come up to the stage, Dr. Berrah, and say a few words?" the president beckoned. I took to the podium. "Actually, Mr. President, I believe that everything has been said." A security guard walked up with a large suitcase and placed it beside me. "The suitcase contains all the money for construction-related expenses," the president revealed confidently through the loudspeakers. For the most part, illiterate workers did not have bank accounts; hence, they had to be paid in cash. A few attendees protested loudly: "Why is Berrah favored at the expense of his elders?" I leaned into the microphone and said, "Mr. President, I wish to thank you for your confidence. I am sure you understand that this is a major undertaking. In my own humble way, I ask that you insulate me from any financial involvement by depositing the funds into a local bank account, and coincidentally, there is a bank president among us. He is a trusted Muslim intellectual who attends Friday prayers at the mosque. I am confident that he wouldn't mind overseeing all financial processes for the entire project. I also recommend that we employ the services of a technical director, someone I believe would be the best man for the job. May I introduce to you Mr. Antoine Cesareo, the director of Grands Travaux and one of the seventeen greatest engineers in

France." The audience applauded loudly. Fired up and animated by the atmosphere, the president took to the podium and spoke energetically: "This does not preclude your responsibility in the adventure, Dr. Berrah." I applauded him and gave a thumbs-up.

I assembled a team of workers from across sub-Saharan Africa, headed by a highly competent foreman from France. We broke ground on the project about a couple of weeks after the town hall meeting and proceeded quickly to beat the deadline. Because of our limited budget, we sought the help of construction companies and received *ex gratia* contributions of equipment, including a tower crane, for the project's duration. The local business community came together to donate all the needed gravel, woodwork, and glass frames. Their commitment and support exceeded my wildest expectations.

I kept a keen eye on daily progress and oversaw the recruitment of various specialty handymen like a seasoned construction foreman. The workers' morale was key to ensuring their efficiency on the job. I urged them to put their heart and soul into the project and led by example by designing the intricate details of the geometrical interior mosaic on the floor and walls. My strict adherence to perfection rubbed off on the crew. For fear of having to redo substandard work, they did their best to ensure that every step of the design phase was up to par with my standards. Our collective sacrifice was a modest gift to Allah. I treated all the workers to a drink and weekly meals on Fridays and brought my wife along every so often to explain the building process. She was always astonished and impressed by the speed of progress, but I said very little to the president because I wanted to keep him guessing until the grand finale.

Plans to install the dome on the minaret had been in the works for some time. The delicate process had to be mapped out strategically with a team of experts to guarantee a foolproof installation. When the long-anticipated time finally came, I was excited and nervous, because I knew that we were inching closer to a successful completion. The tall and slender spire is a typical addition to a mosque. For this project, the structure was designed to be a working minaret. It had a balcony for the *muezzin*, whose chant would call the faithful to prayer. The erected minaret stood at over a hundred feet tall on the corner of the platform of the mosque, and it was symmetrically designed to complete the architectural composition.

The beautiful minaret.

My Love and I joined the few spectators who were already on the scene to watch the dome installation from under a spotlight in the heat of the night. Skilled workers secured a magnificent crescent moon to the large dome and lifted it off the platform with the tower crane. Mr. Cesareo and his team of experts monitored every inch of the nail-biting process, while we prayed for divine intervention to prevent any accidental mishaps. We watched anxiously as it made its way across the moonlit sky, drifting back and forth on the harness, until it was finally placed onto the apex of the minaret with decisive precision.

Everyone breathed a collective sigh of relief and applauded the men. Cheers echoed into the neighborhood, and we rejoiced alongside local residents who had flocked to the site and stood for over three hours to witness the historic occasion. I was so happy that I was moved to tears. I expressed my deepest gratitude to Mr. Cesareo, each member of his team, and all the workers. With the last piece of the puzzle finally fitted in place, the project had come to a successful conclusion in all its glory, bringing everyone a little bit of respite and a semblance of pride.

Riviera Mosque.

I owed a debt of gratitude to the many corporate donors whose generous contributions helped us build the mosque without exceeding our budget. But for Mr. Cesareo, the Riviera Golf Mosque, as exquisite as it now stands, would never have been completed. It remains a gem and a true jewel for the faithful, and the best part is the fact that we managed to complete the project at a modest price. After interacting with everyone on site and expressing our sincere appreciation for a job well done, my Love and I left for the night. On the drive home, I sat silently in the car and reflected on the magnitude of the historic endeavor. Titi beamed with pride and showered me with praises for the successful outcome. "All this would not have been possible without the guidance and intervention of Allah, to whom belongs the glory," we both agreed.

President Houphouët was pleasantly surprised and reacted with utter amazement at the record-breaking construction phase.

"Congratulations," he said. "It has barely been two years!"

"*Merci*," I replied, "but most of the credit goes to Mr. Cesareo. A committee is already hard at work, planning the inaugural ceremony." I knew how important it was for him to preside over the grand opening. When the day finally arrived, most of the leading imams showed up in force with hundreds of the faithful. The extraordinary moment was chronicled in an unforgettable ceremony. The president was the main guest of honor. He delivered the introductory welcome through a wireless PA system, a cutting-edge technological innovation at the time, and served up an eloquent speech about our common faith: "*I cannot emphasize enough, the importance of our service to the Almighty for the general good of all mankind.*"

President Houphouët-Boigny did not just intend to facilitate the economic success of Côte d'Ivoire; he also wanted to nurture the spiritual development of the population, particularly among the youth. Our goal did not begin or end with the erection of a mosque. The objective was to lay a sound foundation for the young intellectuals who populated the Riviera area. We both believed that the mosque had to be led by an imam who was well versed in Islamic theology. Several qualified candidates appeared on the radar, but I ended up selecting Sheik Tidjane Bâ. He spoke Dioula[2] and French and could also express himself in perfect Arabic. But most importantly, his deep understanding of Islamic theology was unmatched. In my opinion, he was the ideal imam with supreme spiritual intellect to nurture the faith. Due to his proficiency and religious qualities, His Holiness Pope John Paul II invited him to join the Assisi ecumenical prayer[3] in Italy. For years, I looked forward to hearing the theme of his *khutba* at Friday prayers, because his profound wisdom helped foster my thoughts. My Love was tangentially affected by those moments when I came home from the mosque and discussed the context of the sermon with her. She appreciated the fact that the spiritual wisdom of the message brought some nourishment to our spirits.

Imam Tidjane Bâ.

The Riviera Golf Mosque reached its maximum capacity for Friday worshippers in only a few months. I began to witness an increase in the number of young intellectuals among the congregation. Religious pride brought them a sense of belonging and an extra spring in their step. The humble, gracious, and extremely considerate Tidjane Bâ was truly an amazing imam and quickly became everyone's favorite celebrant.

He once went on a pilgrimage to Jerusalem and brought back a rosary for my wife, a practicing Roman Catholic. She was pleasantly surprised. A rosary from an imam was a gift so precious and profoundly thoughtful that she continues to cherish it to this day.

"Bonsoir, Docteur." Abdoulaye, a day laborer from the Riviera Golf Mosque project with a reputation for persistence and professional conduct, greeted me as soon as I arrived at my wife's pharmacy on a late afternoon. He stood back nervously and forced a sparkling smile, hoping I would know who he was. I gazed back at his thin, tall frame. *"Ah, bonsoir, Abdoulaye. Comment vas tu?"* I was curious to know how he'd been since the last time we saw each other at the construction site. He was seeking a recommendation letter for a new job. I had grown accustomed to such encounters. In the days after the end of the project, many of the workers in and around the city approached me whenever they recognized my car, and the theme was always about jobs or personal struggles. Several months of long and laborious toiling on the grounds had brought us closer. We felt like a big extended family. I did not hesitate to ask Abdoulaye to come to my apartment at exactly 5:00 a.m., and he wasted no time bringing a couple of his trusted friends along, right on

schedule. Rumors began to spread like wildfire around the day labor community, and before long, many of them came to see me. They queued up at my doorstep, in the stairway, and around the terrace every morning at five, shortly after I was done with my dawn (Fajr) prayers.

My Love and I were living a quiet life in a modest first-floor apartment with lovely views of the Ébrié Lagoon in Cité Esculape, in the Plateau commune. For years, the serenity was fiercely guarded and our peaceful retreat remained undisturbed until everyone suddenly knew where we lived. She had converted the entryway into a flowered terrace and decorated our open patio with colorful hibiscus flowers. The terrace had become a favorite spot of mine to relax and have my morning cup of tea. I quickly turned it into a temporary field office—a meeting spot for the relief seekers and me to engage each other.

After my morning prayers, I appeared with a pencil and paper, pulled up a patio chair, and greeted everyone. "*Bonjour, mes amis.*" They came at me, one by one, or sometimes as a couple. The issues were not limited to job search and recommendations, but also were about economic hardship and personal endorsements. I grappled with the nagging question of how best to help everyone on a daily basis. It was quite a challenge and a constant struggle for me, but I never lost sight of the fact that they were very hard workers. From the moment I hired them for the Riviera Mosque project and got to experience their sense of gratitude for the opportunity to be a part of something special, I knew that they were proud people, but most importantly, they were not looking for handouts. They had come from local and far-away places inside Côte d'Ivoire and from countries in the sub-Saharan delta to seek employment. I was just as committed to their struggle as they were, and they saw that in me.

And so, the routine continued. Like clockwork, they would come to queue up in the wee hours of the morning and wait for me to finish praying. At times, the line extended from my first-floor apartment all the way to the ground floor. They were courteous to each other and kept a respectful distance in the queue to allow some privacy for their peers. I interacted with them for exactly two hours every weekday. On the weekends, no one came to disturb us. As time went by, more and more people who had nothing to do with the construction project came to present me with a variety of issues. I was okay with extending a helping hand to everyone as long as they remained disciplined and took my recommendations to heart. Their gratitude was delivered with deep sincerity and an extension of heartfelt thoughts and prayers, especially among those who received introductory letters from me. The expression of appreciation left me speechless every time. I wished each individual a great deal of luck and watched him or her disappear into the tropical morning dew, hoping they would nail the job interview, maybe secure a permanent one, or at least find temporary placement.

There were certain unique circumstances when I felt the need to help resolve some disputes for the sake of fairness. Even though I hoped to end my early morning commitments at my terrace, there were times when I became a resolute advocate for those who were victims of unjust treatment in labor disputes. I took on the responsibility and made time in my day to visit former employers to address the matter and bring some relief to the workers. My wife was an avid volunteer of her services as well. She was an accredited pharmacist running her own business and told me many times to never hesitate to call upon her if I needed her help. I tried hard to not involve her in what had become an unprecedented labor of love, but at times I had no other choice, and she was more than happy to keep her word. When I sent those who lacked funds to pay for their prescription, they went to see her with a special note from me. Without hesitation, she processed the order and went over the instructions with them.

At times, I did my best to insulate her from the pressures by validating the prescriptions on my own and giving some money to those dealing with urgent medical situations. All in all, my favorite interactions were with the fathers who came to me seeking letters of recommendation to enroll their children in schools of higher learning. I rarely encountered a high school graduate with a low grade-point average seeking entrance into a vocational institution, but it did happen once or twice, and I made sure they got an earful from me before handing them a note.

Out of the many individuals who came to see me on the terrace, the overall majority were genuinely honest and hardworking people. But there were those who came on occasion hoping to take advantage of the situation. I admonished a young man who asked that I contribute to the repair of an air-conditioning unit in his car. "Nonsense. What do you think this is? Don't come here again." I reprimanded him for wasting my time and asked him to be more considerate of others.

I never felt apprehensive nor did I harbor second thoughts about interacting with the group of mostly strangers who came to see me for help. There was just a warm and compelling kinship with everyone. I wouldn't say so for the president's palace commander, General Kouassi, who came to see me one morning out of concern for my safety because he'd heard that I was always "intermingling with all sorts of people at dawn." I thanked him for caring and assured him that all was well; however, I wasn't about to change my routine anytime soon. I couldn't quite understand why he worried about my well-being because I never envisioned a violent attack or robbery. The people needed me to be there for them. When I fell ill at some point and didn't show up on the terrace, the first person in line anxiously rang our doorbell shortly after five in the morning. He knocked softly a few more times until my Love opened the door and apologized for my unfortunate absence. "Please come back in a few days, my friends," she told them. I could hear the instant chorus of well wishes from the bedroom as they dispersed into the morning fog.

I had pondered on a few occasions how I could personally put some of them to work again and convert my benevolent outreach into a real sustainable project for the most competent among them. The only item on my list was a plan to build a house for my wife and me. I owned a piece of land in the Riviera golf area, and I had been saving up to build my dream house, my own Taj Mahal, which I would offer to my Love as a surprise gift. I would call the residence "A Hymn to Love" and have it designed like a classic Italian Palladian villa formed in a U-shaped structure and fashioned after a pink Greek temple, with accents of multiple white Ionic columns. I first saw a villa like that in southern Louisiana during a student excursion, but I was sold by its grandeur when I saw a rendered depiction in the movie *Gone with the Wind*. Pierre Fakhoury would be the architect of choice when the time was right.

Little by little, I inched closer and closer to the design phase after months of visualizing the finished product. When I called on him, I was 100 percent sure of exactly how the design of my dream house would look like. He loved the concept and seemed excited to take on the project. His final design was a well-crafted blueprint projecting my vision in concise detail. I was ready to pay for his hard work, but he handed it to me as a gift from the heart.

It had been months since that day, and the time to break ground arrived while I was still living at the apartment. I hired each and every one of the workers who were involved in the Riviera Mosque project. They were among the lucky few. By then, the lines had softened a bit. The stream of disenfranchised folks had lessened, but they still showed up nonetheless, prompting me to wonder what would become of them once I vacated the premises and settled in on the other side of town, far away from the area. I thought long and hard about a way to help them and decided to direct everyone to meet me in the conference room of the Riviera Mosque, a more convenient location.

Knowing fully well that my imminent transition would have an impact on how I balanced my daily schedule, I began to focus on activating a systemic approach to what had clearly become more of a social welfare program on my terrace. The consistent flow of aid seekers to my doorstep for several months wasn't something I anticipated, nor was it a situation I could sustain as an individual. I moved beyond extending a helping hand to proposing a bill to the president. At the time, both he and I were fully cognizant of the promise of our nation's success and its influence on neighboring countries whose economies were teetering on the brink of collapse. Many day laborers who immigrated to Côte d'Ivoire came searching for a prosperous life, and those who employed the workers benefited greatly from their hard work. I thought it was only fair that the state impose a minor tax levy on employers to help fund a new social welfare system, the Fonds de Solidarité. The objective was to use collected taxes to build vocational institutions and retrain able-bodied workers for the emerging economy. My bill was voted on and adopted as the law of the land to be implemented for the benefit of society.

The hardworking men completed the magnificent villa in record time, and miraculously, the project was delivered under budget. They enjoyed a brief but stable period of sustained employment, which gave them some breathing room and accorded them ample time for reflection. With the new law in place, most of them made appropriate career moves, and the illiterates pursued further education.

To celebrate my wife and show my appreciation for her unyielding support and understanding, I offered a custom-designed solid-gold key as a symbol of my everlasting love. I handpicked some of the workers to stay on as house help and security personnel, and I referred others to a variety of jobs.

I soon embarked on another development project with my dear friend and brother Essy Amara in his hometown. The tiny, sleepy village of Kouassi Datekro in Côte d'Ivoire's Bini region of about two thousand inhabitants was a mishmash of religions, comprising mostly of Animists, Muslims, and Catholics. He had returned from a pilgrimage to Mecca, where he miraculously found himself praying inside the Ka'aba, a most revered shrine, after losing his footing while embedded among thousands of circling pilgrims. A divine premonition inspired him to build a mosque in his hometown, but the council of elders, including his beloved father, advised him to include a rundown Catholic Church in his plans to ensure continuing religious harmony in the community. His wife, a devout Catholic, was pleased to hear the news. He came to see me at home in Abidjan after the decision was made. "My brother," he said, "I need your help to make this happen." I embraced the idea right away. Within days, we went to the town and held court with the elders. We surveyed the site for the two projects—a mosque beside a church—and reviewed our options. He had already donated some building materials for the construction, but we joined forces with the village elders to set up a fund, and we both initiated the seed investment.

When I informed the president about our plans, he championed the vision and pledged his support through a significant contribution to the fund. I was overjoyed by the idea of erecting two buildings for two unique devotions, side by side, to illuminate the beauty of our common faith.

The local village priest, a young Frenchman by the name of Père Alain Derbier, impressed us with his extensive background in construction when he came forward to volunteer for the project. We welcomed the idea and gave him full responsibility to oversee the entire construction. As the country's Permanent Representative to the UN, Essy spent most of his time in New York, and I traveled on occasion for work, but I took on the responsibility of managing both projects. The commitment entailed a whole lot of road trips between Abidjan and the village. I spent several hours of my leisure time at the construction site, working from sun up to sun down, and then I drove back home late at night. The priest tried his very best to keep me in the loop even though it was almost impossible at times due to infrequent phone problems. We used a courier to deliver messages during lengthy periods of communications blackout.

The exceptional opportunity to interact with neighbors from both faiths brought out the best in everyone. All the day laborers worked hard on both projects interchangeably, regardless of their religious affiliations. Everyone seemed eager to bring the project to a successful close. At its completion, we inaugurated the mosque and the church on the same day and organized a major celebration for the entire village. I joined Essy and his family to take in the joyous occasion with everyone. Though he could not attend, President Houphouët-Boigny was very pleased to hear the news. He was extremely proud of the hard workers. I could not stop praising the Almighty for allowing me to witness the exemplary flow of harmony and display of selflessness among the people.

It wasn't very long before an unusually long dry season ushered forth a discordant atmosphere that prompted a surprise visit from the young French priest. He drove all the way to see me in Abidjan to report on rising tensions between Catholics and Muslims in the village. "This was all brought on by the lack of rains," he said regretfully. The residents were in the midst of the worst drought in memory, and members of the Muslim community gathered to lead a special prayer session for the rains to come. Amazingly, during their prayer session rain clouds began to gather, followed by the sound of thunderstorms, and heavy rains began to pour.

Convinced that Allah had heard and answered their prayers, the grateful Muslims planned a thanksgiving ceremony: they would sacrifice four sheep for the village, and they thought it was only fair that the Catholics purchase two of the four. When they approached the Catholic leaders, they refused, arguing that it was a novel ritual that was foreign to their beliefs. I sensed his frustration, but I also understood the mindset of those who were antagonizing his congregants. He stated his dismay over the entire incident in a very composed and reflective manner. "It is my opinion that the Catholics are being forced to participate in an Islamic sacrament," he said dejectedly. I expressed my sincere gratitude to him for taking the time to come to see me and let him know that I sympathized with his point of view. We spoke about the importance of continuous unanimity among the people in the village, which was so prevalent among the faithful during the inaugural ceremonies.

The conversation had a calming effect on him. "*Mon Père*," I sighed. "This is all a simple misunderstanding. I would like to make a contribution on behalf of my Catholic brethren and pay for the two sheep, if that is okay with you." He listened. "As you know, the principle of giving thanks to the Almighty was endowed to us through the teachings of all religions. Sometimes, we differ in the way we give thanks, but we all share one common faith." "Well said," he agreed. I assured him that I was at his disposal to talk about anything, especially matters that caused friction in the village.

"It means the world to me to know that everyone in the village continues to live in peace." He left my house with a little less weight on his shoulders. A few days later, he called to confirm that the village had regained concord and harmony.

President Houphouët-Boigny's dream was to build a basilica in Yamoussoukro with the help of his family and name it "Our Lady of Peace" in honor of the Virgin Mary. Ever since His Holiness Pope John Paul II blessed the cornerstone for the building, shortly before the consecration of the Saint Paul Cathedral in Abidjan, he continued to pray and meditate over the project. I knew how much it meant to him, and I felt his life force whenever he spoke to me about his vision.

Our Lady of Peace Basilica.

From around the world, we faced criticism the moment we broke ground. Throughout the entire construction phase, there were a few ambiguities in articles published somewhere around the globe. For some reason, Western journalists in particular focused only on the monumental size of the proposed building and nothing else. However, critics at the newspapers who authored the numerous articles about the basilica did not sway the president in any particular direction. He looked forward to the completion of the process, and he nourished the deepest wish for a new trip from the Holy Father for the consecration. Mr. Antoine Cesareo, the project's manager who oversaw every aspect of the Pierre Fakhoury masterpiece, immersed himself and committed to safeguarding the architectural integrity of the construction from beginning to end. After five years of meticulous labor, with the utmost attention to every minute detail, the basilica was finally completed and heralded as a pioneer in its capacity, among the best architectural feats ever accomplished on Ivorian soil. Today, the magnificent structure stands as a historical jewel.

Nothing could guarantee the coming of His Holiness. Dissenting voices and critics speculated that there could possibly be some obstacles that might prevent the pope from making the trip. President Houphouët-Boigny was shocked when he learned of the perversion of facts by critics who spread falsehoods, claiming that the construction of the basilica was designed to stop the advancement of Islam in Côte d'Ivoire, but such rumors had not caused discontent among the much larger population of Muslims. The reaction from the Vatican became increasingly reserved, and the coming of the Holy Father seemed to be in jeopardy. The president and I were aware that bad press had placed His Holiness in an untenable position and that the public discourse could prompt him to stay away for fear of inciting the Muslim population and causing friction in the country.

President Houphouët was caught off guard by the intensity and magnitude of the harsh rhetoric that was being espoused by the skeptics. As a concerned Muslim, I finally decided to embark on a mission to the Vatican to wipe away all the disparaging criticisms once and for all. When I arrived, I was received by Cardinal Angelo Sodano, the Secretary of the Council for the Public Affairs of the Church, in the presence of the Ivorian ambassador to the Vatican, Mr. Joseph Amichia.

"*For the Muslims in Côte d'Ivoire, there is nothing too large or too beautiful for God.*" Those were the first words I uttered, in all sincerity, to Cardinal Sodano. We spoke for several minutes and connected spiritually, but the full force of my earnest approach and purity of my genuine disposition resonated beyond any heartfelt words between us. At the end of the visit, he promised to deliver my message to the Holy Father. We were both in awe of the moment. Ambassador Amichia told me after Cardinal Sodano escorted us through the hallways of the magnificent premises that it was highly unusual for him to walk any guest beyond the doors of the meeting room. We took in the jaw-dropping sights of the frescoed Renaissance-age paintings and decorations in the resplendent architectural building one last time.

With Aillot-About, Pope Paul VI, and Minister Usher.

Despite having been to the Vatican a couple of years earlier, I still could not get enough of its majesty. At the time, I joined Minister Usher and Charles Aillot-About, Ivorian ambassador to Italy, for formal talks with Pope Paul VI on opening the Holy See's first Ivorian Embassy. I made sure to visit the Vatican Museum just to admire the impressive array of Renaissance paintings. I ventured inside the Sistine Chapel to view Michelangelo's nine paintings on the magnificent ceiling and trace his depiction of God's creation of the world, God's relationship with mankind, and mankind's own fall from God's grace. I stopped at every painting along the hallways and corridors to peruse priceless gems by Sandro Botticelli, Pietro Perugino, Pinturicchio, Michelangelo, and others. It was an art lover's delight within the walls of a spiritual haven that pays homage to the Almighty.

Cardinal Sodano delivered my message to Pope John Paul II, and it was well received by His Holiness because shortly after my return to Côte d'Ivoire, we heard that the pope would commit to the trip. Within a few weeks, his plane touched down in Yamoussoukro for the historic occasion. I went to greet him at the presidential palace on the eve of the consecration and held his hand in my palms. "*Your Holiness, I am Ambassador Ghoulem Berrah. I was the one who came to the Vatican to affirm that the Muslim community would be more than happy to see you at the basilica. I'd like to welcome you to Côte d'Ivoire, and I wish to extend to you my sincerest gratitude for making the long journey on this historic occasion.*"

Greeting Pope John Paul II.

I mingled with the select few who had arrived for the reception. The pope's exceptional tenderness could be felt in an atmosphere of intense spiritual energy. After endless months of construction amid all the media frenzy, the day had finally arrived, and we all took in the memorable minutes of mystical indulgence in the presence of His Holiness, who sat humbly in our midst, smiling modestly, and receiving everyone in his good graces. He showed subtle signs of fatigue from a whirlwind trip that had taken him across the Mediterranean to three East African countries prior to arriving in our beloved Côte d'Ivoire. The president engaged him in a quiet conversation for about half an hour before he was escorted to the waiting papal limousine for the drive to his private residence on the basilica compound.

As soon as he left the reception, my wife and I went to see a group of imams around town to solidify their commitment to attend the consecration. Every Muslim leader in Côte d'Ivoire had been invited to the ceremony, which was planned for September 10 in the year 1990, and most of them had arrived in the day. Monsignor Mullor flew into Abidjan from his station in Geneva a few days earlier and stayed at our house. We drove to Yamoussoukro together to ensure that the on-the-ground logistics were in order. He was always tremendously helpful and ever ready to lend a helping hand. We went to tackle our duties separately and planned to meet up for dinner later that evening. I owed him a debt of gratitude for his moral commitment, something akin to a natural trait in an unrelenting and vibrant personality that reigned supreme from the moment we broke ground on the project until the very end.

After a hectic series of meetings with the imams, Titi and I were assured that they would all attend the consecration. We breathed a sigh of relief only when we were convinced that our outreach and overtures to the Muslim community had paid off in the name of peace and continued harmony between the two major religions. Monsignor Mullor met us for dinner at the Hotel Président. The restaurant was packed mostly with dignitaries and others from the pope's entourage.

I told him, "*My dear brother. I would like to convey a message to the Holy Father. Please get the word to him that I am assured of the attendance of Côte d'Ivoire's imams for tomorrow's event. I have the full commitment of each and every one.*" The words flowed from my lips to the happy ears of Monsignor Mullor, who had barely sat down. "Ah, Ghoulem. This is very, very important." He excused himself and scurried off to invite Joaquín Navarro-Valls, the pope's personal spokesperson, to our table. With a high level of astuteness and disciplined restraint typical of the Opus Dei, Mr. Navarro-Valls looked into my eyes with curious expectation. I delivered the same message to him. He thanked me, shook our hands, and promised to notify the Holy Father.

Pope John Paul II began a powerful homily with one memorable sentence: "*I would like to thank the imams of Côte d'Ivoire for their presence in this basilica and for attending the ceremony. I welcome each one of you.*" When the cameras of the world were finally focused on them in the basilica, viewers around the world were almost blinded by the sea of white *boubous* gracing the pews. The historic scene transformed our critics into instant admirers. Lest we forget, peace and harmony had won over the naysayers, and the whole world had become a platform for unity among humans in celebration of our common faith.

My Love has always respected the precepts of Islam, and I have also respected those of the Catholic religion. Hence, I have never experienced the feeling of having a faith that differs from hers. We will forever continue to share our common faith in one God.

The month of Ramadan was always as meaningful and exciting to my wife as it was to me. "*Chéri*, please remember to bring home a calendar from the mosque today." Those words had been repeated by her, each year, at almost the same time, over decades. She remembered to remind me at least a week or two before the beginning of the season. For years, Titi maintained the same practice of ensuring that she stayed abreast of my routines to help me break fast. Even when I lagged behind the start time for prayers, she was always quick to give a tender reminder to let me know that it was time for my Dhuhr[4] or Asr[5] prayers.

During the holy month of Ramadan, Muslims usually begin to fast from predawn and break the fast at sunset. Right on time, my table was always perfectly laid out with a selection of mouthwatering dishes like Ivorian cream of rice, coffee, milk, dates, *burek,*[6] and my all-time favorite Aïn Beïda dish, *chorba frik*[7] She prepared the meals and waited patiently to eat with me after I broke the fast. She even kept me company when I woke up to have a late-night snack. With a little help from my sisters, she managed to stock up on most of the base ingredients: fresh green *frik* and other essential produce varieties that were native to Algeria. *Zrir,*[8] a key ingredient for breakfast concoctions at the end of Ramadan, was a key addition to her inventory. At times, she served a delicious couscous or *tajine*[9] with prunes. I looked forward to the last course of desserts after a hearty meal.

My Love knew that the most difficult aspect of Ramadan had very little to do with abstaining from eating or drinking. It was a deeper commitment that enforced to the faithful the importance of self-discipline. Speaking ill of others, uttering offensive words, commenting negatively, or acting in a way that could be perceived even in the slightest terms as causing harm to one's neighbor are actions that must be resisted. The main objective of every believer is to undertake a spiritual awakening through prayers and good deeds in order to strengthen the soul and be closer to the Almighty.

Titi also maintained some cohesion with me during Ramadan. We fasted together for the first three days, and then she joined me to fast once a week, including the twenty-seventh day—the Day of Destiny. I spent the holy month in the small French-Swiss border town of Annemasse and worshiped at a local mosque from time to time. Always mindful of the importance of dialogue between the faiths, I insisted that my wife invite the priest from her parish to break the fast with us. Though soft-spoken, the young priest, Père Alain Viret, had an upbeat personality and was very curious about world affairs.

As a matter of fact, he was seduced by the idea of celebrating the spiritual feast at our house. I welcomed him at the front door on a mild spring evening and led him into the living room. "Thank you for having me, Dr. Berrah. I am delighted to make your acquaintance. I can hardly wait to learn about Islamic customs." "You are welcome, *mon Père*. It is a pleasure." Titi walked in with some dates and milk. "It is time to break the fast," she said. Seeing the puzzled look on his face, I felt the need to explain the tradition. "We usually break the fast with something sweet to compensate for the low blood sugar levels after a full day of going without eating. Please enjoy, and excuse me while I go and say my sunset prayers. We will have dinner as soon as I am done." He nodded. "But of course. Please take your time."

He was in deep conversation with Titi when I returned. I overheard him highlight the similarities between Ramadan and the Lent observance by people of the Catholic faith. "Essentially, the objective is to get closer to God. However, for us Catholics, we indulge mostly in prayers and penance, whereas Muslims tend to submit physically in many ways. The intensity of fasting is a telltale sign of their very own unique approach."

Over dinner, he spoke about the need for all humans to take heed and fulfill in their hearts the teachings of their religion. He hoped to develop a forum for Christians and Muslims to meet and interact for better understanding of the commonalities of faith. He was an interesting character who soon found out that the subject matter was very dear to my heart. My entire life had pivoted naturally at the intersection of religious harmony among all faiths. "Well, it has been a lovely conversation in great company," I said. "But unfortunately, tradition is beckoning yet again. I have to take my leave and go to the mosque." Titi chimed in, "*Ah oui*. It is time for him to go." The priest was gracious. "I understand. *Merci beaucoup*, Dr. Berrah. It has been an honor. Hope to see you again very soon to continue our insightful conversation." It was part of my routine in the holy month to go to the mosque and pray the Taraweeh[10] after breaking fast. He remained with Titi and they spoke in depth about faith and servitude to the Almighty.

The Holy Qur'an must be read by the faithful in its entirety during the month of Ramadan. Each year, Titi never missed the opportunity to ensure that I completed the process. She always stayed up late at night until I returned from my Taraweeh prayers, and she would muster up enough energy to ask for an update, sometimes prompting me to recite parts of the holy verses to her. Eid al-Fitr, the festival of breaking of the fast, is one of Islam's two most important celebrations, and it begins at the end of Ramadan. Prayers and festivities at mosques around the world mark the culmination, but the faithful are especially prayerful and charitable at the end of the fasting season.

Although Muslims from around the world are expected to visit their local mosques to affirm their undying dedication to their faith, the Annemasse Mosque was never large enough to accommodate everyone. Frequently, organizers would bus people to a larger venue elsewhere. I had come to expect this to be a normal annual routine for several years, but I had no idea that my Love had quietly been contributing money to fund the transportation until a member of the organizing committee said something to me about how much she was appreciated. I was pleased but not surprised, as it was in her nature to give of herself without drawing attention to her deeds. For years, I thought that I was the sole beneficiary of her undivided attention.

Never could I have imagined that she had been going out of her way to shower my Muslim brethren with so much selfless kindness. My Love has always been more than a devout Catholic who has dedicated herself to the faith with the utmost devotion. She is a magnanimous individual plain and simple. She worries about the comforts of others and acts in accordance with the altruistic principles of our common faith.

My wife receives the Holy Communion from Pope John Paul II.

Titi's undying wish was to receive the papal benediction from Pope John Paul II himself. Though His Holiness had previously sent the apostolic blessing to be delivered at our wedding by Monsignor Kutwâ, I promised to do whatever I could to make her wish come true someday. Not very long after we tied the knot, I asked the Ivorian ambassador to the Vatican, Mr. Amichia, to help us gain audience with the pope. The tireless and dedicated civil servant was more than happy to deliver. Weeks later, Titi and I arrived at the Vatican as scheduled to meet with Pope John Paul II for the very first time.

With my wife, Ambassador Amichia, and Pope John Paul II.

The momentous occasion left me with an indelible and profound impression of the pious yet meek pope. I was captivated by his innate ability to interweave strength and tenderness with unbridled warmth and humility. Embodied within his saintly persona was a man with a great sense of humor. It was an easy interaction for several minutes, with my wife and I listening intently to his every word and immersing ourselves in his divine, wisdom-filled oratory.

When we were done praying, he handed a rosary to my wife, and then he gave one to me. Our hearts were forever stirred with unmatched emotions after the encounter.

My wife receiving a rosary from Pope John Paul II.

OUR COMMON FAITH – A Plea for Interfaith Harmony

Receiving a gift from Pope John Paul II

My Love and I have forever cherished our yearly anniversary. We always look forward to the day like no other, and she asks her priest for a thanksgiving mass, no matter where we happen to be. In Geneva, we pray at l'Eglise de l'Immaculée Conception, the enchanted church in nearby Vésenaz, where we tied the knot. In any other part of the world, she locates a Virgin Mary–affiliated church and asks for a special mass. I have never had second thoughts accompanying her to church, or to the ICAO[11] chapel, and never once have I hesitated to celebrate Sunday mass with the president at his chapel, because I believe that no matter how or where we pray, we all reach the same God.

Leaving San Marco Basilica, Venice, on our twenty-fifth anniversary.

Some twenty-five years ago, we were exiting the ICAO chapel after our mass when we met a Saint François Xavier Holy Sister from the Sainte Marie High School in Abidjan. She recognized Titi from her high school days at the affiliate school in Neuilly, near Paris. When Titi introduced us, she asked if I wouldn't mind visiting the local school someday to give a presentation on interfaith marriage. I was honored but hesitant, because I did not think I was qualified to speak about the subject. I thanked her graciously and told her that I would ponder the proposal. *In my heart, I never saw any difference between my wife and me. We were two connected souls just living our faith.*

I learned to appreciate the spiritual depth of the sisters at the Saint François Xavier Community, and I valued the importance of their apostolate because of my wife, who maintained strong ties with her former school. She subscribed to and read the alumni quarterly newsletter religiously. It wasn't until we settled into our retirement in the United States that she suggested I read an article in one of her newsletters. I was struck by the content. My mind traced the roadmap of what seemed to be a common goal in the pursuit of peace. It then occurred to me that the students who had come from all over the world were taught to live together in a climate of mutual respect, with a deeper understanding of the Christian, Muslim, Jewish, Buddhist, and Hindu religions. A light bulb illuminated my thought process, and it dawned on me why the sister had extended the invitation to me in Abidjan some twenty-five years earlier. I placed the newsletter down and asked Titi to set up a meeting with her former tutors on our next trip to Paris. They told her that they would be more than delighted to receive us for a casual meeting of the minds.

We called from Geneva in the summer and went to meet them for a hearty breakfast at their Rue de Poitiers home in a quiet residential part of the Parisian congregational quarters. It was an honor and a pleasure to finally meet the two Holy Sisters. Sister Jacqueline d' Ussel was a former director of the collective Sainte Marie institutions around the globe and one of the great influences in my wife's early educational experience. She embodied exceptional personal traits: a very open-minded, strong, and forthcoming individual with much profundity. She was with Sister Odile de Vasselot, also quite a remarkable and dynamic woman—a past member of the French Resistance during World War II. She was the founder and former director of Sainte Marie High School in Abidjan.

Despite juggling many responsibilities in their daily routines at the apostolate, they were full of life. Nature had been kind to them over the years; hence, it was impossible to detect any signs of aging in either of them. There was a light behind the flame that kept them animated, and it illuminated the room during our time with them. I congratulated them for their innovative approach to youth education and for encouraging religious tolerance. They were humble and soft-spoken, but with an astuteness that carried over and filled the atmosphere with the spirit of service to others.

We shared many philosophical and religious ideas and engaged their sensibilities in a vibrant and jovial conversation that at times veered into deeper discussions about Côte d'Ivoire, mostly touching on the heydays of President Houphouët, and the future of the country. They were aware of the ongoing political turmoil in the country and affirmed to us that they prayed each day for the people to pull through. Titi and I expressed our concerns about the uncertainties. But for me, the situation had become an especially painful reflection because I was witnessing the daily deterioration of our hard work in three-dimension. We all stressed the need for peace to prevail in the world and bonded on sentiments of harmony with unfettered justice for our beloved Ivorian brethren in the days ahead as they prepared for highly contentious elections. We thanked them for their service and dedication and promised to stay in touch often.

Vacationing in Hawaii.

On Christmas, Easter, and other major Christian holidays, I accompanied my Love to church. Some years, we flew directly out of New York at the conclusion of the annual UN session in mid-December to take in the warm and sunny tropics of the Pacific Islands and celebrate Christmas at a midnight mass in Honolulu. If we happened to be in a Muslim country, I found a church for her to celebrate Sunday mass. In Annaba,[12] our nephew Salim always volunteered to escort her to the Basilica of Saint Augustine in Hippone.[13] I looked forward to visiting my old friend Cardinal Léon-Étienne Duval at the Notre Dame d'Afrique Basilica whenever we celebrated mass in Algiers. He lived on an adjacent compound a short walk from the basilica. The cardinal, a Frenchman, had been a friend of Algeria during the lengthy war, having protected several freedom fighters from the colonial forces. He remained an influential and revered personality known for his bravado. The locals gave him the moniker Mohammed Duval.

My friend Essy Amara, my wife, and Imam Tidjane Bâ.

He continued to live in the country even after independence and throughout successive administrations, but he expressed grave concern for the direction of the country during the early 1990s. Those were tumultuous times in Algeria, and I prayed for the Almighty to allow peace to endure over all our troubles. Our house in Abidjan was open to all imams and priests. Monsignor Mullor entrusted Opus Dei, the pope's prelature of the Catholic Church, to me in spite of my faith, shortly before he left Côte d'Ivoire. As a consequence, I met Monsignor Alvaro Del Portillo, a holy man and companion of Saint Josemaría Escrivá, the founder of Opus Dei, as well as his successor, Don Javier Echevarría Rodríguez. Each encounter left me more impressed. The depth of their spirituality was interlocked with all that I knew about my faith, life's principles, and man's ultimate quest to sanctify the ordinary life for the glory of God.

Imam Tidjane Bâ and Monsignor Mullor.

After Monsignor Mullor's departure, his successors in the Apostolic nunciature continued to nurture our friendship. As far as the charming Polish priest Monsignor Janusz Bolonek was concerned, our house was a peaceful haven, second only to the nunciature. He called my wife on many occasions to ask permission to visit us whenever he hosted guests from the Vatican. Titi was always more than delighted and honored to receive everyone for lunch. I also looked forward to those times as an opportunity to mingle and never hesitated to take my leave from the president to help accommodate the guests. A sampling of hors d'oeuvres and appetizers usually followed a tour of the villa, while my Love treated everyone to cultural classics and traditional Ivorian dishes.

Carving some fish for Monsignor Bolonek.

Their favorite main dish was peanut stew with rice, slices of boiled ripe plantain, and yam. Lamb *méchoui* stuffed with couscous, a popular North African delicacy, was always par for the course. As usual, prune *tajine* and a large selection of seasonal tropical fruit with French pastries capped off the lunch. Those were fun times. We ate and relaxed to meaningful discussions about everything, even sharing a few laughs when we caught ourselves getting too serious.

Monsignor Bolonek and I bonded over time. From the very beginning, he was captivated by our interfaith marriage. He pushed our conversations about Islam and Christianity to deeper levels and highlighted the similarities among all religions. Theology, Muslim dogmas, and so forth had embedded truths that revealed such parallels to the believer. Monsignor Piero Marini, the master of ceremonies for Pope John Paul II, was one of the many notable Vatican visitors to our home when he came to Abidjan to prepare for the consecration of the basilica. After Titi and I thanked him for overseeing the massive consecration preparations, he expressed himself with remarkable humility and indulged us in a witty display of pure modesty. "I feel culturally enriched, even though I have only been here a few short days," he said. "You seem to have adapted very well," I replied. "*Merci*, Dr. Berrah . . . *et merci à vous*, Madame Berrah, for the warm hospitality. Indeed, I feel truly pampered."

With Father Touzet, Monsignor Alvaro del Portillo, and my wife.

I grew accustomed to being in the company of the Holy See diplomats. At times, I longed for our interactions because they always demonstrated to me the highest of standards and were extremely effective at every facet of diplomacy. Monsignor Giuseppe Bertello, an overtly friendly and humble man with a selfless personality, succeeded my dear brother Monsignor Mullor as the Holy See's representative to the UN in Geneva. Having been charged with overseeing human rights abuses around the world, he and I were constantly discussing ways to tackle the most disturbing issues in specific countries. His practical approach and remedies were personal attributes that drew me to him, and I reciprocated by introducing constructive measures to solve some of the problems.

I emphasized the need for more diplomats from developing countries and decided to reach out to Monsignor Mullor to discuss the possibility of an agreement with the Holy See to open the doors to an internship program at the Vatican for young Ivorian diplomats. Much to my surprise, I found out that as a prerequisite, each aspiring candidate had to be a priest, and they had to go through a selection process in order to be admitted to the Pontifical Academy, of which Monsignor Mullor later served as president. Upon completing the course at the academy, graduates were then required to follow the normal process that took them through the various ranks as a diplomat of the Holy See. It was interesting, but either way, I was disappointed to discover that the opportunity to participate in the program was not available to our Ivorian diplomats.

On occasion, I felt the need to get away from diplomacy and my hectic schedule—to have a more in-depth reflection about the meaning of my actions. These feelings took on a sense of urgency around the holy month of Ramadan, and I usually felt a strong desire to go on a pilgrimage to Mecca. By the grace of the Almighty, I was fortunate enough to record nine such pilgrimages to the Hajj, one of the five pillars of Islam. This is a required commitment for every Muslim to undertake at least once in their lifetime. It is also recommended that all who make the pilgrimage should in turn help others who lack the means to do the same.

At the heart of the pilgrimage is the Ka'aba, known to the faithful as the House of Allah. This most venerated Muslim shrine sits at the center of the Holy Mosque in Mecca. The Prophet Ibrahim built the shrine and many centuries later, it was rebuilt with the help of the Prophet Muhammad (S) to encapsulate the Black Stone. It serves as a focal and unifying point among the faithful, which is why Muslims around the globe turn their compasses toward Mecca during daily prayers to ensure that they are facing the Ka'aba from wherever they may be.

As destiny would have it, I had the immense grace and distinguished honor to be among a select few to participate in the cleaning of the Ka'aba on two memorable occasions. The monument is covered by a *kiswah*, a gold-embroidered black silk cloth with adorned verses from the Qur'an. Traditionally, a piece of the Kiswah is given to each individual who participates in the cleaning ritual. The two kiswah pieces that were given to me at the end of my sacrifice are my most cherished prized possessions.

The pilgrimage to Mecca is from the eighth to the twelfth day of Dhu al-Hijjah, the twelfth and last month of the Islamic calendar. Because we use a lunar calendar, our dates are eleven days shorter than the standard Gregorian calendar, and accordingly, the Gregorian date of the Hajj changes from year to year.

The Hajj is associated with the life of Prophet Muhammad (S) from the seventh century, but the ritual of pilgrimage to Mecca dates back thousands of years to the time of Prophet Abraham, known by Muslims as Ibrahim. At the same time each year, pilgrims by the hundreds of thousands from all over the world converge upon Mecca during the week of the Hajj.

Like my fellow pilgrims, I embark on my spiritual journey in a special seamless white garment, an *ihram*—required clothing to enter Mecca. The custom signifies a renunciation of the outside world for a more humble and pious life. I am always filled with strong spiritual emotions whenever I make my final entrance to the Haram, a designated area encircling the city perimeters measuring about three miles wide and eighty miles long. Each year, pilgrims follow in the footsteps of the Prophet to formally declare their devotion to Allah the Almighty.

The Hajj begins with the welcome Tawaf[14] and the Sa'I[15] ritual once we enter the Holy Sanctuary (al Masjid al Haram), right foot first, through the Bab Al-Salam gate. At the Holy Mosque, we are led in prayer by an imam who chants verses from the Holy Qur'an in a voice so unique and powerful, it sends chills down my spine and literally moves everyone to tears. We then proceed to the small village of Mina to spend the entire day in meditation and prayers in solidarity with the Prophet's ritual. Before sunrise the following day, we head to the Plain of Arafat to meditate and pray on our feet atop Mount Arafat, another solemn and poignant experience for those of us who are moved to tears during the prayer ritual of Prophet Muhammad (S).

We spend the night in reflection under the open skies of the Muzdalifah valley just like the Prophet. Upon awakening in the wee hours of the morning, we collect pebbles for the stoning of the devil ritual and return to the town of Mina to cast the stones at the three walls of Jamarāt. The faithful believe that Jamarāt is where the devil failed in his attempt to persuade Ibrahim to sacrifice his son.

It is at Mina that we commemorate the sacrificing of lamb in a synchronized ritual with Muslims around the world. The feast of Eid-al-Adha represents the sacrifice of Ibrahim. To show gratitude to Allah for his generosity and blessings, most of the meat is given to the poor. Those who are unable to participate in the sacrificial ritual make monetary donations to the needy. The second Tawaf takes us to the small hills of Safa and Marwah for a walkabout ritual that begins and concludes with the drinking of water from the Well of Zamzam.

By then, the state of *ihram* is presumed to be fulfilled, except for two more days of ceremonial stoning. We head to the Holy Mosque in Mecca to complete the farewell Tawaf. I felt lighter and spiritually cleansed, but I always had a tough time with my emotions on the day of departure. For pilgrims, the Hajj is not complete until we go to pray at Prophet Muhammad's (S) tomb inside the Al-Masjid al-Nabawi Mosque in Medina, the second holiest city in Islam. The mosque was built by Prophet

Muhammad (S) and refurbished centuries later to include the renowned Green Dome, a unique fixture over the Prophet's tomb. I usually began my pilgrimage in Medina and found the memorable experience to be one of reinvigoration and purification; hence, year after year, I could not wait to do it all again.

On a couple of occasions, I went to Mecca at the invitation of the Saudi royal palace. But for the most part, I embarked on each of my nine pilgrimages on my own accord and did so without complications. I remain eternally grateful for being so fortunate, because many of the faithful do not always complete the process. Ever mindful of the Muslim calendar, President Houphouët-Boigny always offered pilgrimages to a select group of Muslims each year.

Though my Love and I were inseparable, the Hajj kept us apart, but by the grace of the Almighty, we managed to embark on our very own unique pilgrimage to Jerusalem—the cradle of Christianity, Judaism's most divine sanctuary, and one of Islam's holiest cities. We planned to meet in Tel Aviv after one of my pilgrimages to Mecca. She traveled from Geneva to Zurich, then endured a thorough security check before boarding her flight. We both arrived a few minutes apart and greeted each other at the airport on a beautiful Friday afternoon. For me, the restful weekend was all I needed after my physically demanding pilgrimage, in spite of the unique spiritual fulfillment. On Sunday morning, we were picked up by our chauffer and shuttled to church. We both grew very fond of Elie, the friendly Sephardic Jew from Morocco, and decided to make him our designated driver for the duration of our stay.

The beauty of Jerusalem is revealed in the early morning sunshine, a city draped in white cliffside homes. Varieties of pale dolomitic limestone, common in and around the city, had been used in the construction of buildings since ancient times. When we came back to the Mount of Olives Hotel, where we stayed, we inquired about finding a tour guide, and by sheer coincidence were introduced to an Algerian. Ibrahim was a very animated and dynamic person, fluent in Hebrew, Arabic, and English. Years before he was born, his grandfather had come to the British colony of Palestine after a pilgrimage to Mecca and decided to settle down in Jerusalem. We felt right at home with him from the moment we began sharing our trip objectives. For five days he would be at our disposal, and he would be responsible for a memorable interfaith pilgrimage. "Firstly," I told him, "my most distinguished wish is to pray at the Al-Aqsa Mosque. And for my wife, a pilgrimage to the Basilica of the Holy Sepulchre would be in the highest order." We discussed other key must-see destinations in the Holy Land and narrowed them down to a solid itinerary. He knew of all the religious sites.

    On the first day of our pilgrimage, I rose from bed in the early dawn, full of anticipation and looking forward to my maiden pilgrimage to the Al-Aqsa Mosque. Ibrahim was already waiting in the lobby to greet me. Not long after I left, my Love began her morning in the exquisite gardens of the hotel, meditating and reflecting on the experiences of Christ and his Apostles by the Mount of Olives. We took a short trip to participate in the Fajr prayer at the magnificent Dome of the Rock. From there, we headed to the Al-Aqsa Mosque in Old Jerusalem. According to Muslim doctrine, the mosque completes the fifth pillar of Islam. We went inside to meditate for a while before attending the Dhuhr prayer. My heart was overjoyed. I was completely overwhelmed by the weight of the moment, even as I focused deeply on a passage in the Qur'an about the mysterious journey of the Prophet Muhammad (S) from the place I stood in prayer. It was a blessing to have been among the few Arabs to achieve that particular milestone.

When we returned to the hotel at the end of prayers, my Love was ready to get going. We asked Ibrahim to join us for a light lunch before embarking yet again for a trip to Old Jerusalem. The driver pulled up to the pretty square at the entrance of the old town, known as the Damascus Gate, and we walked past the Al-Aqsa Mosque again to show the site to my wife. We stopped at the ancient ruins of the Second Temple, the revered Wailing Wall—Judaism's holiest shrine. It lays at the foot of the western side of the Temple Mount, beside the mosque. The area was bustling with activities, and we saw many Jewish faithful bowing their heads rhythmically in prayer at the wall. Flocks of people stood in line and moved a step at a time to take turns to meditate. We moved across an old narrow road to get to the house of Pontius Pilate, where Jesus Christ was put on trial. There was so much energy around us from the moment we set foot in the area. It felt like a spiritual awakening.

Undoubtedly, the time has come for us to reflect on our common faith in one God, the one who revealed Himself to mankind in three different ways right where we stood.

When we left the house of Pilate, we paced through the pavements of the old picturesque town and made our way toward the Basilica of the Holy Sepulchre. I went into the Mosque of Omar, across from the basilica, to meditate for a few minutes. Walking in the footsteps of the caliph in a mosque that was built within range of the basilica was an experience to behold. The mere historic significance made me shudder as I replayed the story in its context: Omar, the caliph, was at the basilica when he realized that it was time for the Islamic prayers; the site's administrator invited him to pray inside the basilica, but he wisely refused because he did not want his Muslim brothers to take over the holy place in the future. He stood and cast a stone and went to pray where it landed. Hence, a small mosque bearing his name was erected on the very site where he prayed.

As we were entering the basilica, I worried about how my wife would react. She seemed at peace. According to Christian teachings, we were treading lightly on the grounds venerated as Golgotha, the Hill of Calvary, where Jesus was crucified—also known to contain the tomb where Jesus was buried. The sepulchre remains a paramount destination for many Christians and a most important pilgrimage site. When we finally made our entrance, my Love was suddenly overcome by emotions. She couldn't hold back her tears, and I was profoundly affected by her. I grabbed and held her hand tightly to soothe her. We stood side by side in the heartland of Christianity, and with each breath, her soul lent credence to the deepest bonds of her faith. After a couple of hours, we returned to the hotel to unwind the emotions of our first day.

Our second day was marked by a visit to Bethany—the home of Martha, Mary, and their brother, Lazarus. "It is said that Jesus arrived in Bethany six days before the Jewish celebration of Passover," Ibrahim told us. "Martha served dinner in Jesus's honor, and Mary poured perfume on his feet." We reflected on those words and walked across the compound to the tomb of Lazarus.

The Basilica of the Nativity in Bethlehem was next on our list. I was astonished to see for the first time the segmentation of the various Christian faiths—branches of the Orthodoxy, Catholic, Protestant, Methodist, etc. Making our way down two flights of steps to the Grotto, we passed the Altar of the Nativity and arrived at a holy recess with a fourteen-point silver star, surrounded by Latin inscription, proclaiming the site as the birthplace of Jesus. It was a stirring encounter for my wife, who was once again moved to tears as she stood transfixed at the exact spot where Jesus was born. *Where else does one get the power to experience all of this over and over again without going numb?* I wondered quietly. We maintained a silent vigil and exited after a couple of hours. The vendors outside the compound showered us with bargains on religious souvenirs, a welcome sight of ease and comfort. We indulged them for a while until it was time for my Dhuhr prayers at a nearby mosque.

The dry midafternoon heat was enveloped by soft breezes and fragrances of summer. Dominating the distant city skyline of Hebron, Al-Haram Al-Ibrahimi Mosque, Islam's fourth holiest site, seemed closer than we thought. We cruised for several minutes down historical roads before we finally pulled up to what is believed to be Abraham's sanctuary and the Tomb of the Patriarchs. For a thousand years, the mosque has been a consummate interfaith pilgrimage site as the resting place for the Prophets Abraham, Isaac, and Jacob and their wives, revered equally by Christians, Jews, and Muslims.

We experienced firsthand the tension between Jews and Muslims in the once peaceful region. The Israeli army was at the mosque's entrance in full force to ensure that the flow of pilgrims moved along peacefully. We came face-to-face with the charged atmosphere for the very first time, providing a reality check, but we chose to meditate on the tomb of the father of all believers rather than allow ourselves to be absorbed by the melee. I followed our guide, Ibrahim, to an area in the southeastern section for the Asr prayers. My Love went on a sightseeing tour that took her to an octagonal room with the cenotaphs of Jacob and Leah, then past a synagogue beside the southwestern wall where the faithful stood in silent meditation. *Into all its tenderness, our once-in-a-lifetime journey carried us into the cradle of our common faith, uniting us as one people.*

We took in the scenic sites en route to Jerusalem, basking in the multiplex of beautiful sunset radiance that soon revealed another mosque in a heavenly setting by a desolate roadside. The ancient structure was born out of the remains of an older mosque that had undergone rehabilitation. The driver pulled over for Ibrahim and me to go inside and pray the Maghreb. For five days, he found a mosque for me every time I needed to pray. Back on the road again, we had a lively conversation. Ibrahim, a real angel and a great find, talked to us about the hidden gems in the Holy Land, and Elie, the soft-spoken driver, shared his sentiments on religious diversity. My Love had an insightful take on the matter, wondering how such an awesome opportunity to harness the power and culture of rich religious diversity could go untapped.

At the hotel, we felt the heaviness of tension that had gradually permeated the blissful night and made its way into the restaurant to disturb the serene atmosphere. Unbeknownst to us, there was a brewing Palestinian revolt in the not-so-distant future. We overheard a couple of Arab waiters at the restaurant speaking openly about the intolerable situation. This was my first contact with Palestinians on their native soil. The writing was on the wall.

On day three of our stay, we drove from Jerusalem to Ramallah, the place where Joseph and Mary discovered the absence of the child Jesus when their caravan came to a rest stop. They went to look for him and found him teaching in the temple among the doctors of the law. Ibrahim explained to us that at the time, Ramallah was a hub and a mandatory stop for caravans. We then moved on to Emmaus, where Christ met some of his own disciples who walked with him without knowing who he was.

At the site of Jacob's Well in the province of Samaria, I was astonished to see that the four thousand-year-old well remained intact and fully functional. The history of Samaria harkens back to a time when Samaritans could not interact with Jews, yet Jesus surprised a Samaritan woman when he asked for a drink of water from the well. "You know," Ibrahim said, "there are still Samaritans living in the area." "Oh, really?" we chimed in unison, totally amazed. "Yes, of course," he replied. "Would you like a visit?" "We would be more than delighted to meet a Samaritan in the flesh," I said. We crossed the street to a small apartment building. When he tapped on the door, a middle-aged man greeted us with a smile and became pleasantly chatty. We could tell that he and Ibrahim knew each other.

We entered the home and relaxed on a sofa in the living room. In line with tradition, our host served some local home-brewed coffee and welcomed us. The male companion who joined us was animated and friendly. Titi and I enjoyed their insightful stories about Samaritan culture, which interestingly enough had transcended the fade of time to entrench itself in modern-day practices. Samaritans continue to live reclusive lives in their very own unique community. We thanked our hosts for their graciousness and memorable hospitality.

We left and drove to the Sea of Galilee, parked a few yards from the beach, and walked toward the shore. While Ibrahim narrated a passage from the Gospel, describing Jesus walking across the body of water, we paused for a moment of reflection and cast our eyes across the sea. As we gazed at the distant horizon, we felt the occasional gusts of the moisture-laden breeze caressing our faces. My Love was overcome with emotions. I held her hand firmly, and we walked back to the car.

A few miles down the road, we stopped at the Mount of Beatitudes, where Jesus delivered the Sermon on the Mount. We got out of the car to admire the lush greenery for a brief moment and drove a little farther down to view Mount Tabor from a distance. For Catholics, the textual passages in the liturgy that day were about Mount Tabor and coincidentally, we happened to be at the site on that particular day. My Love seized the moment to reflect on some passages of her faith before we sped up the road and headed to Nazareth, our final stopover for the day. Just about a few minutes into our drive, we decided to stop briefly at the site of the Wedding at Cana while we were still in the province of Galilee.

In Nazareth, the town where Jesus spent most of his childhood, we were surprised to see a very modern and robust city. My Love later expressed to me her disappointment after our visit to the Basilica of the Annunciation. Neither she nor I had been aware of the fact that the church, which was built over the Crusader and Byzantine foundations, had been demolished in 1955 for the construction of the present-day church. She was particularly dumbfounded because she expected to see a site that was reminiscent of the historical venues on our list. For my part, I realized that our guide might have spared us the unfortunate stroke of serendipity had we bothered to ask a few questions beforehand. Nonetheless, we scouted the premises, tracing a path into the vast upper church, which had been decorated with mosaics of the Virgin Mary. My Love excused herself to pray at a nearby altar. As soon as she was done, we walked down to the lower church in the Grotto of the Annunciation, where the angelic announcement to Mary is believed to have occurred.

She paused once again for a few minutes of meditation. Our trip back to Jerusalem was a long one, but we had many interesting conversations to keep us occupied.

As usual, our guide awaited us in the lobby on the morning of our fourth day. We invited him to sit with us for some coffee and went over events from the previous day. High on our list for that day was a visit to the Old City of Jerusalem for souvenir hunting. From the Damascus Gate, we mingled with many shoppers and walked into some of the small shops along the cobblestone streets. Though I could express myself in Arabic, the few Palestinian shopkeepers who detected my accent were curious to know my country of origin. When I explained to a vendor that I was Algerian and a former FLN combatant who also happens to be an Ivorian diplomat, he showed us a lot of hospitality and invited us to sit for some coffee. Some family members from the back room soon joined our conversation and expressed their joy at seeing us.

We moved along to an adjacent shop and were again invited to sit for more coffee. But soon enough, we were joined by a small group of shopkeepers who converged around us. Most of them spoke openly and poured out their hearts to us, complaining about their brothers in the Arab countries who had abandoned their cause. "As far as we are concerned, Israel is here to stay," a vendor who had just joined the group spoke louder than the rest. He was echoed by a barrage of vociferous sentiments and statements coming at us one after the other: "We are asking our Arab brethren to recognize Israel, because this is the only way for them to gain the entry permits, which will enable them to come and see us and help us free ourselves." "We feel as though we have been forgotten and they don't even recognize our very existence." "You, my friend, are the only one who has paid us a visit in a long time." "We don't even have a passport, hence we are stuck here, deprived of our freedom to move around freely." The encounter amounted to an educational moment for me. I saw it as an affirmation of the importance of dialogue as the best and only way on the path to achieving peace.

At each stopover, vendors spoke openly about their plight, and we perused souvenirs, gladly picking up some rare items along the way. When we returned to the waiting car, Ibrahim and I strolled off to catch the Dhuhr prayers at the Al-Aqsa Mosque. We joined my wife later to embark on our planned visit to Jericho. Parked beneath a tree alongside a busy street in the small town, we went to see a sycamore fig tree, where our guide recounted a verse from the Gospel. He told us about a tax collector named Zacchaeus, a short man in stature who was hated by the Jews because he worked for the Romans. He had climbed up the sycamore fig tree so that he might be able to see Jesus as he approached the town. When Jesus reached the spot, he looked up through the branches, addressed Zacchaeus by name, and asked him to come down, for he intended to visit his house. Onlookers were amazed by the fact that Jesus, a Jew, would dishonor his reputation by being a guest of a tax collector.

From where we stood, we could see the Jordanian border. I wondered how the West Bank, a tiny slit of landmass, was at the center of so much turmoil in the region. We could also see the River Jordan, where Jesus was baptized by John the Baptist, whose father Zakariya is a known prophet in the Qur'an alongside John. Zakariya's role as one of the men of God is frequently referenced in many verses of the Qur'an. We followed along the river's western border and stopped to watch it converge with the Dead Sea.

From the shoreline of the Dead Sea, we watched the sun emerge from the shadows of Mount Nebo. Jews and Christians believe that the Prophet Moses, to whom the Almighty had given the Torah, was buried on the mountain but that his final resting place is unknown. My wife and I went to dip our hands in the sea to experience its density and high salinity. It seemed at first glance that there was an oily tinge on the surface. We both felt a strange sensation, somewhat oily to the touch, but oddly enough, there was no such residue on our hands. "This is an awesome work of nature," Titi said, and I agreed. "As part of their tradition, some rabbis purify themselves in the Dead Sea before the Sabbath," Ibrahim revealed. We left the area and headed toward Jerusalem. Back at the Mount of Olives, he led us to the Pater Noster Church, where Jesus taught his disciples the Lord's Prayer. We were taken in by the multitudes of gorgeous roses in the beautiful courtyard, the pillars and arches, and the imposing neo-Gothic style of architecture. Our focal point was the cloister, decorated with tiled panels of the Lord's Prayer in several languages. Everything was definitely unique in the Holy Land.

At the end of our day, we sat in the hotel lobby with Ibrahim and discussed our calendar for the conclusion of the pilgrimage. My Love wanted to join her fellow Christians and walk the path of Christ on the "Way of the Cross," starting from the house of Pontius Pilate to the Holy Sepulchre. I wanted to attend the great Friday prayers at the Dome of the Rock and take part in the Asr prayer for the last time at the Al-Aqsa Mosque. After organizing our morning program, Ibrahim graciously left us.

We woke up early in the morning, clearly energized and extremely excited to see the holy sites around the Mount of Olives. After breakfast, we could hardly wait to get started. We went to a small church behind a huge wall, commemorating the place where the disciples brought the donkey on which Jesus rode triumphantly into Jerusalem. Christians honor the event by celebrating Palm Sunday every year. We passed by the Zion Gate and went to the crest of Mount Zion, sauntering past the partial remains of an ancient building known as the Cenacle, the site of the Last Supper, where Jesus first introduced the Eucharist, commonly known as the Holy Communion. I watched my wife affirm her dedication at the site for a moment. She paused to offer an earnest prayer in silence. Jews know the site as the final resting place of King David.

Our next stop was the Mosque of the Ascension, which is sacred to Christians and Muslims, known as the place of Jesus's ascension into heaven. The site contains what is traditionally believed to be the last footprint of Jesus on earth. Beside the mosque is a small chapel that was taken over after the fall of the Crusader kingdom by Salah al-Din in the twelfth century and transformed from a Christian church into a mosque. There is an underground tomb near the entrance that is venerated by those of the Jewish faith. We stood still and meditated at the junction where the three major religions converged upon one another and debated among ourselves about why mankind continues to be preoccupied with religious differences rather than finding the common ground where we can all relate.

For my Love and me, this has always been commonsensical and never a mystery to us. We have continuously lived our lives as devotees to our personal faiths, always knowing that the love of the Almighty is limitless and without boundaries. I have by no means attempted to convert her to Islam, and neither has she tried to convert me to Christianity. The world as we have come to know it has become a place that yearns for a true understanding of the faiths.

We went to see the Tomb of the Prophets Haggai, Zechariah, and Malachi (a popular pilgrimage site for Jews), located on the upper slope of the Mount of Olives. A beam of sunlight permeated from above and traced its way into the dark catacomb of arguably one of the holiest mountains in the world. It was as if the Almighty was shining his divine light and beckoning to the faithful. In the midst of the surreal scenery, a Hasidic family smiled at us and wandered into the tunnel. We moved past ancient olive trees with two thousand-year-old roots and crossed into the Garden of Gethsemane, right next to the Basilica of Agony. Christians believe that the roots are symbolic witnesses to the emotional suffering and betrayal of Jesus.

The Church of the Assumption, believed by most to contain the Tomb of the Virgin Mary, was next on our list. We strolled along the foot of the Mount of Olives and made our way down several steps in the dimly lit church to get to the tomb. My Love has a very special place in her heart for the Virgin Mary, to whom she looks for spiritual guidance. She stood silently in the dark and shadowy crypt, and we breathed a heavy fragrance of incense. I meditated as she slowly caressed her rosary. Though we were captivated and in awe of the ambiance, she was on a unique spiritual level, lost in powerful prayers and deep reflection. I glanced over at her and felt every ounce of her energy. After many minutes of extraordinary silence, I held her hand and we made our way out of the crypt.

Ibrahim wasted no time letting us know that the Virgin Mary, mother of Jesus, was taken by Saint John the Apostle to Turkey, where she lived in a stone house on Mount Koressos until her Assumption. The site is both a Catholic and Muslim shrine. We went a little farther down the road to the edge of the Jewish cemetery and were soon rewarded with the best views of the old part of Jerusalem. I became increasingly emotional as the hour of my last great prayer in Jerusalem drew near.

Our final pilgrimage day was slowly coming to a very insightful and enlightening end. I really looked forward to my last day of prayers at the Dome of the Rock with so much zeal and spiritual focus. I was already in a state of meditation when we arrived, and my prayers were very intense. Following the conclusion of the imam's oration, we returned to pick Titi up for the three o'clock commencement of the Via Dolorosa (Way of the Cross) at the house of Pilate. Ibrahim and I escorted her to the meeting place and left her with the Christian faithful. We hastened back to the Al-Aqsa Mosque just in time for the Asr prayers.

During the Muslim call to prayer, we could also hear the Christian procession praying loudly as they made their way past the mosque en route to the Holy Sepulchre, while at the same time the Jews prayed at the Wailing Wall. Together, all the prayers of the various faiths, emanating in unison, rose toward the sky. A sign of our common faith in one unique God.

I couldn't help but think of a verse from the *surah* AL-MA'IDAH 5:48 in the Holy Qur'an: "*Unto everyone of you have we appointed a different law and way of life. And if God so willed, HE could surely have made you one single community; but in order to test you by means of what HE has vouchsafed unto you. Vie then, with one another in doing good works. Unto God you all must return, and then HE will make you truly understand all that on which you were wont to differ.*"

As soon as we completed our prayers, we walked back to the Basilica of the Holy Sepulchre to meet my Love at the exit. It was shortly before the Sabbath was to begin, and it was also time to part ways with our guide. We thanked him for his masterful teachings and expressed our regrets for the quick passage of time. He shared our feelings for an enlightening experience. I exchanged information with him and promised to get in touch in the very near future. Because of the Sabbath constraints, our Jewish driver did not have enough time to take us to our hotel and make it back home in time. We asked him to drop us off at the Damascus Gate.

Within a few minutes, an unmarked car pulled up to us. "*Habibi*, you want a taxi?" the driver asked, using the Arabic term for "friend." "Oh, yes, yes," I responded. "You are not a Palestinian, *habibi*. What are you doing in Jerusalem?" We had barely sat down in the car. "On a pilgrimage with my wife, *habibi*," I told him. He began to talk about the Israeli-Palestinian conflict. We spoke for about twenty minutes. "I am very well acquainted with Arafat. He is like a brother to me," I said. He acknowledged with a nod. Seemingly at ease with me, he felt more comfortable expressing his political views. We arrived at the base of the Mount and drove slowly up the winding road to the hotel entrance. "With your permission, I would like to pick you up tomorrow and take you to a secret location. I am certain you will appreciate what you see." I did not give it a second thought. "Sure, why not?" I agreed. "It will give you an opportunity to see firsthand and allow you to assess our situation in these occupied West Bank territories," he said. When we came to a stop, he refused to take any payment.

He picked us up in the morning. After about an hour's drive through isolated mountainous terrains and desert roads, he rolled downhill and dodged some massive potholes before coming to a stop on a desolate road. "We have to walk the rest of the way," he explained, obviously concerned about my wife's ability to hike with us. I asked Titi if she was okay with a trek down the slopes. "*Je préfère rester ici.*" She was such a trooper. She agreed to sacrifice her safety and wait in the car, alone in the desert, in the middle of nowhere. I saw her take out her rosary to assure me that she was in good company. I planted a kiss on her forehead and disappeared with him through the canyons. "It is a difficult slog for a woman," he said. It seemed that way. The ground was filled with stones and gravel spanning a curvy downward incline. "We did not come prepared for a hike," I told him. We passed through some very narrow valleys and navigated carefully across a few steep gorges to get to a well-hidden training camp.

There were over a hundred young and seasoned fighters on site. They demonstrated an impressive determination to sacrifice their lives for their freedom—a willingness to be among their brethren, united and dedicated to the cause. Each and every one of the young men I spoke to assured me that they stood committed and poised to fight for their liberation, saying, "We stand ready to rid ourselves of this unbearable occupation and form an independent Palestinian state." I listened to their heartfelt remarks and promised to relay the message to Chairman Arafat.

We left the camp and returned to reunite with my Love about two hours later. She was a bit nervous and agitated when I saw her. She had been wondering what to do in the event I didn't come back. "I thought you would only be gone for no more than thirty minutes," she said. "Very sorry, *mon chéri*," I apologized, acknowledging my recklessness. "I was really taken in by an evolving situation and lost track of time." Nonetheless, I was very relieved to see her too. The encounter occurred in August of 1987, just months before the first intifada. It was then I realized that the volatile situation in the occupied territories was on the brink of a massive flare-up. We said very little during the hour-long drive back to Jerusalem. I mostly reflected on the surprising experience and the long road ahead to achieving a sustainable peace. At the hotel's entrance, we bid farewell to the young Palestinian and wished him well.

"All thanks be to God for guiding us through this momentous and spiritually rewarding pilgrimage," Titi said. She breathed a fitting sigh of gratitude as soon as we closed the door behind us. "Indeed, my Love, *Alhamdulillah*." We paused and began to pack our belongings. I woke up within a few hours to pray at dawn and joined my wife for Sunday mass at the beautiful Basilica of Agony, within walking distance of our hotel. We returned to find our driver waiting to take us to the Tel Aviv airport. The days had gone by very fast, it seemed. When he dropped us off at the curb, we expressed our sentiments and parted ways, hoping to soon return to the Holy Land. For five days, we immersed ourselves in a spiritual excursion that reawakened our core fundamental beliefs. We felt rejuvenated and more grounded in our common faith.

The city of Geneva seemed so far away from the Holy Land, but in reality, it made for a perfect transition due to its serene atmosphere. We rested at home for a few days and returned to Abidjan. In the coming days, we shared the highlights of the trip with President Houphouët. He was particularly taken in by my unexpected adventure to the training camp and suggested I go to Tunisia to share the experience with Chairman Arafat.

I still yearned to complete my knowledge of all revealed religions. After honoring an invitation to a Shabbat dinner by my Jewish friend Melvin Cohen and his family in Tucson, I purchased a book on the symbols of Judaism. Melvin, a religious man, was also involved in teaching the scriptures at the University of Arizona. When we arrived at his charming home on campus, we met his wife and father-in-law, who greeted us in French. Much to our surprise, he was very fluent in the language. His wife was high-spirited and sociable and got along very well with Titi. We were soon joined by their little boy, who was quite polite. The couple did their very best to make us feel at home. When the time was right, they led us to the powder room, where we took turns to wash our hands. The table in the living room was set beautifully with two candles. Mrs. Cohen gave a quick orientation about the significance of the candles: they each represented one of two commandments—the first, in remembrance, and the second, in observance of the Shabbat. The ritual was performed as a way to profess one's faith and follow the example of the Lord, who interrupted the process of creation on the seventh day, the day of the Sabbath.

Mrs. Cohen lit the candles before sundown and waved her hands over the flames after ceremonial rites, and she welcomed the Shabbat with a blessing recitation. Melvin took over and recited some more prayers. They sang some verses from the Psalms, and we joined them in spirit amid the pious atmosphere.

The meal was served with slices of *challah*, a specially blessed Shabbat bread, representing the symbol of *manna*. "It is believed that the *manna* fell from the sky onto the desert," explained the father-in-law, a former Auschwitz inmate. Mrs. Cohen served up an exquisite dinner. We relaxed and engaged in small talk with her father, who shared some harrowing details from his time at the infamous Nazi concentration camp. He revealed a tattooed serial number on his right arm, and I told him I was sorry he had to endure so much pain and suffering. Both Titi and I remained transfixed for several minutes. We all shared his gratitude to the Almighty for surviving the camp. His poignant stories stayed on my mind for a while. It was a deep and meaningful learning experience.

I had read a couple of books on Judaism, but I had yet to come across certain aspects of religious traditions, but through my many friendships, I was given an opportunity to learn something new on occasion. When Irving and Audrey Greene invited us to celebrate two bar mitzvahs simultaneously in Florida, we did not know what to expect. The grandfather, a World War II veteran who had served in the US Air Force, was celebrating a renewal of his bar mitzvah, and at the same time his grandson was about to celebrate his first. In Jewish tradition, once a boy reaches the age of thirteen, he becomes a bar mitzvah and goes through a rite of passage in which he transitions from not understanding the Torah to ultimately being considered old enough to begin to understand. Among some Jews, a man who has reached the age of eighty-three will customarily celebrate a second bar mitzvah. The logic being that, in the Torah, a "normal" lifespan is seventy years old, therefore an eighty-three-year-old becomes thirteen again in a second lifetime.

My wife and I accompanied the Greene family to the synagogue to witness the beautiful ceremony for the first time in our lives. One after the other, we watched and listened attentively as the rabbis took to the bimah[16] and delivered some powerful passages from the Torah. I was struck by the depth of the readings of goodness, love, and all the precious values that are prevalent in all religions. "If the Jews applied the precepts of the Torah, the whole world would be changed for the better," I commented passionately to my wife at the ceremony's end. The teachings I derived from my experience were also applicable to Christians and Muslims in the principles of their faith. I have since concluded that I prefer the company of a good Christian or a good Jew to that of a bad Muslim.

Many a time, the topic of religious diversity would become the centerpiece of my conversation with my dear Vietnamese friend Dr. Tran. He was raised a Buddhist. I had gained some insights on Buddhism in China during my FLN student years. That was long before our paths crossed. I knew that Vietnamese Buddhism was similar to Chinese Buddhism, but through our conversations, I learned that their practice has elements that can be traced to Japanese Zen, Tibetan Buddhism, and another form known as Amitabha, or "Pure Land," Buddhism. Just as Muslim children in my native Algeria are often raised in Qur'anic schools, most Buddhists in Vietnam belong to the Mahayana schools. I came to admire how much Dr. Tran's culture and thinking was influenced and shaped by his Buddhist faith. As far as he was concerned, his faith was a way of life that emphasized disconnection to the present. The main holy book, the Tripitaka, was translated from an ancient Indian language that was very close to Buddha's native dialect. In the book, it is written that people reap today what they have sown in the past.

What really impressed me about Dr. Tran was his enduring patience. This was a key component of his personality. It was at the core of his disposition, having been instilled in him from a very tender age. His wife was much the same way too. Tucked in the corner of their yard was a small greenhouse with a nursery of orchids. She tendered to the plants with the utmost care and forbearance. Some orchids flourished well, others stayed bloomless for years, and although she thought she might never see the rewards of her hard work, she was satisfied with the belief that someone else would enjoy the fruits of her labor someday, long after she leaves this earth. Titi and I often marveled at her selfless inclination to be a steward of good so that others may reap the benefits and perhaps continue the good work. We could relate because it was in perfect synchronicity with the spirit of service to the Almighty. Our own faith teaches us that sacrifice is indeed a moral obligation that is looked upon favorably by Allah. The foundation of all religions rests upon the concept of morality. The sincerity in leading a religious life, the quest to follow the righteous path, and a desire to practice honesty in judgment, sincerity in speech and in all of one's actions, including aspirations, are intrinsic values that correlate to our faith. The precepts of nurturing a healthy spiritual state of mind are necessary to foster genuine sincerity in prayer and meditation. Our fellow Hindu brethren share similar patterns in worship. What I have seen among adherents of every religion are the commonalities of our specific beliefs and ultimate objective. But there is also a spiritual reality that transcends our finite human experience. The role of religion, therefore, is to serve as a roadmap to guide us by emphasizing the moral commandments and encouraging humans to follow a better path, to work for peace in the world, and to be tolerant of others.

My wife and I share a common faith in God's plan for us. Like the vast majority of people, we were hoping to be blessed with children. When we realized that God's plans for us would be different, we did not fall into despair. Instead, we reflected on the wisdom of the words of Monsignor Mullor: *"Having children is a blessing; not having any is also a blessing."*

We became very close with the monsignor a few decades ago. Throughout the years, we took turns visiting each other regardless of where we happened to be. When he was at the papal station in Geneva, he was kind and generous enough, going beyond the call of duty, to drive several miles to bring the Holy Communion to my wife at the Clinique de Genolier every single day for a month. We visited him in the Baltics and journeyed to

Mexico to see him once. He was the first nuncio to be assigned by the Holy See to the three Baltic states after the fall of the Soviet Union. When I accompanied him to the Lithuanian capital of Vilnius to help with his move into a new sanctuary, I warmed up to the local Secretary of the Nunciature, Monsignor Mario Cassari. During the few days I spent at the complex, I quickly gravitated to him because his technique reminded me of the level of artistry I aspired to achieve at Indiana University.

Monsignor Justo Mullor Garcia.

I never associated priesthood with artistic talents, but he was a master of surreal abstract paintings, and I took a liking to his creative touch. Moreover, his abilities went beyond the depth of most abstract painters, and when he dedicated two of his prized paintings to me as a gift, I was honored. The portraits transformed his communist experience into a unique artistic interpretation, influenced by colorful details that chronicled an inimitable political journey. He took me on a tour of the underground painting scene in a different part of the city, where I came across multiple spectacular masterpieces by great painters who used their art to depict life in a state of captivity behind the Iron Curtain. Later that day, when we had dinner as usual with Monsignor Mullor, I was tempted to ask my hosts about the permanent diet of baked or fried cabbage with cabbage soup, which had been par for the course ever since I arrived. They both nodded to acknowledge me and began to eat. I shrugged off my own question and joined them. Months afterward, my wife and I managed to get together with Monsignor Mullor in Estonia for the Christmas holidays. Our friendship blossomed deeply over the years, and he joined us on memorable vacations at multiple destinations. To this day, he remains our spiritual brother.

Having the capacity to acknowledge God's presence in our lives has enabled my wife and me to accept the premise that to not have children is to also respond to another one of God's plans. Hence, our fate will serve its purpose by giving us the opportunity to overcome the role of our core biological family and cast a keen eye on the children of others in order to nurture their needs. We have many godsons and daughters around the world, to whom we continue to give our undivided attention. Every single one of them is our source of joy, and this also is a blessing.

Although not having children has placed us at the disposal of those who providence has positioned in our path, I have always known that not having children has also allowed me to continue my commitment toward achieving peace in search of a better world. I could not begin to imagine facing the torment of being a parent who must abandon their children to fulfill another duty.

For my wife and me, God's purpose is also reflected in the variety of his creation. The beauty of his creation resides in the diversity of human beings whose skin colors are akin to a palette, ranging from milky white to ebony black. It would have been easy for the Almighty to create us all in uniform colors and sizes, but instead, he chose to ensure that each person is a reflection of the unique power of his creativity. Unfortunately, there are still many people who waste a lot of time failing to appreciate the uniqueness of each other. For his part, the Almighty uses each of us in the same way a man and a woman would contribute the XX and XY chromosomes to give birth to life.

Despite our many imperfections and failures, my wife and I will always invoke the power of our unique God in all aspects of our lives. We have embraced the force behind all creation as a source of inspiration on a daily basis as we continue to appreciate every waking moment. All my life, I have tried my very best to serve the Almighty, and in so doing, I have been blessed and he has illuminated the road on which I continue to travel with but one desire: to communicate these sentiments to others who seek happiness in God's guiding light and reaffirm the belief that our religion shall not divide us. For it is God we seek, and in that quest, spirituality must unite us in *one common faith*—and *HIS* world shall be a better place for all humankind.

Endnotes

[1] A state agency that oversees major construction projects.

[2] A Mande language spoken in Burkina Faso, Ivory Coast, and Mali.

[3] The first World Day of Prayer for Peace, held in Assisi, Italy, organized by His Holiness Pope John Paul II.

[4] Noon prayer. One of the daily prayers performed by practicing Muslims.

[5] Afternoon prayer. One of the daily prayers performed by practicing Muslims.

[6] Family of baked or fried and filled pastries made of a thin, flaky dough.

[7] Gravy soup (chorba) with green wheat (frik).

[8] Mixture of sesame seed, dried fruits, honey, and butter.

[9] Meat or poultry stew combined with vegetables, flavored with spices.

[10] Special evening prayers performed during Ramadan.

[11] French acronym for Catholic Institute of West Africa.

[12] Annaba: city in the northeastern corner of Algeria.

[13] Hippone: the imposing hill over the city of Annaba.

[14] Ritual walk counterclockwise seven times around the Ka'aba in meditation.

[15] Moving back and forth seven times between the hills of Safa and Marwah.

[16] Platform in a synagogue from which the Torah is read.

Epilogue

After circling the world forty times, I took the decision to retire and settle down in the United States, having resigned from my tenured professorial commitment at Yale University a little over three decades earlier to answer the call of Africa. My purpose was to go back and serve the continent. I was obligated to work hard for a better world. My most esteemed wish was to support Africa's development and create conditions to allow every newly independent country to excel among the concert of nations. Reaching that milestone would not only enhance relations among all nations, but more importantly, it would motivate the youth of the world to interact in harmony. The rapprochement, I believed, would serve as an augmentation of consciousness and mobilize future generations to embrace the spirit of oneness on planet Earth. We sail on the same boat, though each of us disembarks on a different day and hour to join our maker.

Memories of my African experience emanate from a mixture of complex outcomes and constant frustration in the struggle for economic development. In the immediate aftermath of colonial withdrawal, the continent was caught flat-footed in the middle of the Cold War, with many nations becoming a pawn in the political ideologies and mounting tensions between the Eastern and Western blocs. Worst of all, our economic oppression was fair game, and our raw materials were in play. Price fluctuations and currency devaluations were a standard daily occurrence and a major concern for leaders all over the Third World. Plans were hampered by uncertainties of the times, and developmental projects were derailed.

I often thought about one of the great American presidents, my personal favorite, Abraham Lincoln, who, upon winning reelection, stated in his inaugural address on March 4, 1865, "*It may seem strange that any man should dare to ask a just God's assistance in wringing their bread from the sweat of other men's faces.*"

More than five decades after independence, many African countries are lagging behind a majority of nations in Asia. While most in Asia are seeing exponential and rapid development, the overall majority of Africa's sovereign countries are struggling to gain traction. Failed policies by corrupt governments have led to a vicious cycle that has forever anchored down the mobility of progress. We see the economies of nations with the world's largest natural resources dipping into the red and staying there for decades on end.

Rather than place their faith in commodity exports alone, it would be wise for today's governments to learn from the mistakes of the past and diversify their economies, empower their citizens with knowledge of science and technology, and design an environment for innovative minds to excel. The young generation needs solutions at home. They are hungry and determined to succeed, but opportunities must be made freely available, and access to quality education and global interactivity in the cyberspace must become a standard norm. We live in a world that is getting smaller by the day, and a paradigm shift is forcing change at a pace never before seen in human history. If

Africa seizes on its potential, it would go a long way to solving its own problems.

My diplomatic experience in global politics has helped shape my worldview. The role of the US in finding solutions for the world's problems cannot be denied. One of the reasons why I decided to retire and settle down in the US was because she wields such sphere of influence around the globe. All eyes are on this nation. After getting my education in America and becoming a lecturer, the transformational experience became a part of my very being. No society embodies so much unity in such a diverse way.

I have always treasured the fact that the entire world seems to exist in the

United States, and as a workaholic, I came to appreciate the values of hardworking Americans, most of whom are to be commended for taking absolutely nothing for granted and for believing that success is borne out of hard work. Not long after President Houphouët passed away, my wife and I left the shores of Côte d'Ivoire for a tranquil neighborhood in a Denver suburb. We became American citizens, quickly immersing ourselves in society and engaging in our civic duties like most decent Americans.

Although imperfect in its democratic experimentations, it is still the people who give mandate to their representatives to act on their behalf. Even if some in Congress may be animated by noble ideals, they are sworn to work to fulfill the agenda of their constituents. In many instances, however, they yield to the influence of campaign financiers and lobbyists in their decision-making, and as a result, commonsensical measures are not implemented. President Barack Obama had to deal with a partisan Congress that placed ideology of party over the interests of the nation and obstructed his entire agenda in an abhorrently divisive way.

As a country of immigrants, where many come to ply their trade, perfect their craft, and deliver unmatched transformative innovations to the world, the US is the place where each person's ingenuity is embraced with an open mind. The world remembers a country that dispatched its military to fight two wars on two occasions to liberate Europe and defend the free world. But the quagmire in the Middle East has long been the most challenging foreign affairs conundrum the country has ever faced. Due to America's ever-evolving political balancing act and perceived bias toward Israel in the quest for a sovereign Palestinian state, the world has resigned itself to deal with a status quo that is begging for a revolutionary change. At every turn, the US continues to squander an opportunity to be a genuine broker—a neutral force for good, a nation that must lead the Palestinians and Israelis to peace.

The world's leaders could use a moment of reflection to channel the wisdom uttered in the words of President Lincoln at his second inaugural address: "*With malice toward none, with charity for all, with firmness in the right as God gives us to see the right, let us strive on to finish the work we are in, to bind up the nation's wounds, to care for him who shall have borne the battle, and for his widow and his orphan, to do all which may achieve and cherish a just and lasting peace among ourselves and with all nations.*"

As a diplomat, I risked my life in the pursuit for peace, working with organizations like the ICIPP and the PLO. I sat in think tanks with the likes of General Peled and Dr. Isam Sartawi and searched for ways to bring Israeli and Palestinian representatives to the table. Dr. Sartawi was assassinated by his

Palestinian brothers because of his pursuit for peace with Israel. Prime Minister Rabin, who once told President Houphouët that he would embark on the road to peace as long as Chairman Arafat agreed to take similar steps, was also assassinated by an Israeli extremist. Though the road to peace has been painfully littered with dangerous outcomes, achieving the ultimate goal in the very near future would go a long way to honor the heroic efforts of those who have been martyred.

America has its share of domestic problems, some of which can be attributed to the anachronistic policies that at times inhibit the flow of progress and upward mobility. Perhaps unbridled capitalism might be to blame, due to a perceived lack of fairness to everyone, no matter what their background, race, or creed. The downside of capitalism can be equated to the belief that money buys happiness. While it is indeed a very good thing to be a great businessman and make lots of money, a misguided desire to achieve riches at all cost can lead to conceited patterns of thought and in many ways induce people to turn their backs on those who may be less fortunate. It seems as if the entire world has descended into the depths of materialism, and henceforth, it has become increasingly difficult to operate in harmony with transcendental truths. We are succumbing slowly but surely to that which is materialistic and becoming worshippers of matter. We are at risk of losing our spirituality and turning our backs on the true meaning of happiness.

The soul of the modern man yearns to indulge in all his desires, and it tempts him to embrace materialism, which has now replaced religion to rule over his mind and spirit. The belief that there is no other goal in life than to accomplish material success is something without truth or merit, and like a prisoner, such belief entraps one to become oblivious to their true sense of self and makes them lose their spirituality. A man therefore runs the risk of losing any sense of warmth from his human nature, thus making him seem indifferent to others.

This happens at the top of the ladder, from the boardroom to the executive branch, from upper management to the corridors of politics. For instance, whenever the issue of minimum wage comes up for discussions in Congress, the topic produces divergent views along party lines. Certainly, jobs must be created, but workers must be paid a decent salary for a hard day's work. Those at the top tend to forget that this is a necessary component to alleviating poverty and hardship.

Racism is still rampant in our country, despite the denial by some. When Obama was elected, there were many who claimed that the historic moment was proof of the end of racism. I cried on the night he won the election. Like others from my generation who have suffered in their hearts after witnessing firsthand the tyranny of segregation, I am not nostalgic, nor do I yearn for a return to the tenebrous past. Though significant progress has been made since my days at Yale in the 1960s, we still have a long way to go. Recurrent incidents taking away lives of innocent individuals are painful and troublesome.

Race and culture are real forces in American life because they are entrenched in politics. Take, for instance, the process of filling out an administrative questionnaire at your local government office, where one is almost always asked to specify their ethnicity. It is a requirement that at first seems to be rooted in archaic processes from bygone days, hardly a twenty-first century custom. As a matter of fact, identifying one by their race is a procedure that was invented for statistical data-mining purposes. Though this simplistic strategy has served society by ensuring that today's legislatures can mine data to support their ability to conduct a more reliable census count, even identify and log migration patterns of the various ethnic groups, still, records from their findings are being used to determine how to regulate and control the allocation of federal funds to the states. As with any well-intended practice, politicians tend to find a loophole in the system to exploit. The policy of gerrymandering has become standard practice. In this sinister strategy, districts in minority communities are redrawn in such a way that their votes will not make a difference.

A society's racist shortcomings are not by default. The tendency to segregate by race and count individuals by their ethnic and cultural heritage is, by definition, prejudicial and divisive. It promotes a spirit of "us and them" and carries forth a conception of "rich neighborhood versus poor neighborhood," and alas, the public systems in those poor communities are deprived of vital resources for lack of representation. It's no mystery why so many feel left out of the system or do not feel like they stand a chance in achieving the American dream. My hope is to one day see the tail end of the plague of racism as it is extracted from its very roots, leaving in its wake the birth of a new society—the ultimate utopia.

No one would argue against the fact that not everything should be decreed by law. Most decisions can be motivated by our very own genuine aspiration to do what is right for each other— to speak out and to stand up for others, without being indifferent to anything. I place my faith and trust in the youth to meet the challenges by saying no to hatred and doing their very best to make the world a better place. While getting rid of clichés and by thinking with their own heads, they might reveal the best part of themselves. Only then will their vital impulses and their creative genius take over. Peace starts with each of us; it should not be a dream. We must make the pursuit of peace our constant reality. Young people have their own way of seeing things. They are all connected through social media and want more interaction to understand the rest of the world. They seem poised and ready to undertake actions and get to the root of problems. It is imperative that America remains fully conscious of her responsibilities, be full of wisdom, and lead by example instead of continuing to impose our rules on the rest of the world. When we attempt to force change by manipulating one group over the other just to protect our interests, we are failing as a nation. Today's youth are a different breed. They are intent on changing the world by being fair and transparent.

In light of my faith, and knowing fully well that each one of us has a specific mission to fulfill during his or her lifetime, I ventured to put all my heart in whatever I tried to accomplish at every single moment, and I embraced all humans as unique in the eyes of the Almighty. The attributes that define me are faith, honor, duty, love, justice, peace, and dialogue. These are characteristics that can move mountains. While we are still sailing in a common vessel known as planet Earth, I believe in my heart that I have accomplished my life's mission. I can now sense that the time has come for me to get ready to disembark and go to meet my Creator.

Epilogue

Forty years of divine grace.

By the grace of the Almighty, our love has lasted through the test of time.

Acknowledgments

As the widow of my beloved husband, His Excellency Dr. Ghoulem Berrah, I am honored and duty-bound to write these few words of appreciation on his behalf:

First and foremost, my most sincere and heartfelt thanks go to Mr. Nana Yalley for managing to convince my late husband that his memoir was worth writing, and assuring him that at least, more than one individual would be interested in reading about his life. It took some nudging and some divine intervention, but Nana's persistence paid off. In reminding my husband that the odyssey of a purposeful life was a story worth sharing, his words would not be lost on my husband's conscience, as he conveyed to him that he would otherwise have to explain his failure to complete this fated duty when he meets his maker. My husband, who was always consumed by the need for world peace, long envisioned setting up a nonprofit interfaith foundation. He began to ponder the merits of producing such a book for a humanitarian cause, and became deeply animated by the thought of making a modest contribution toward promoting peace.

On a momentous day, he awoke in the wee hours of the morning and prayed the Fajr prayers. As he gazed across the ebbing ocean, charmed by the rising sun on the brilliant horizon, he reflected on his life's mission and began to record his thoughts on the mini tape recorder that he received from Nana. With his fountain pen, he wrote the first few words of a memoir that had been etched in his psyche his entire life. This became his routine in the months ahead.

When my Love asked me to proofread his material, I gladly accepted, without knowing that I would discover some very interesting aspects of his life that had been buried deeply in his memory, some of which were new revelations to me. I became an avid reader of every chapter, with the exception of the one titled "Murky Waters of Love," which he secretly kept at bay, knowing fully well that I would have vetoed the story of our very private life. I was so captivated by his storytelling capabilities that I wondered at times if I had lost all sense of objectivity, an attribute that has served as the golden rule of my life.

This became his very last project. It was an assignment that he took just as seriously as anything else he had been involved in. He entrusted Nana to direct and oversee the project and to review the minutest details of his manuscript until the book was published. I did not know that in his heart, he was quietly preparing for his departure. He invited Nana for some midafternoon tea at our home and organized a long working session immediately after. Several memorable pictures and documents were laid out in rows across the large conference table, deliberately sectioned to synchronize the various chapters of his planned book. Missing were the decades-old pictures of Chairman Mao Zedong, Vice Chairman Li Shaoqi, and Premier Zhou Enlai, which he'd searched feverishly for, to no avail. The pictures had circulated among friends during interactions over the years and had been lost along the way. In an effort to reassure himself that we were on the same page, he revealed his choice for the book's cover picture. He wanted to ensure that we knew exactly what to do just in case. The Lord called him not long after he had completed his manuscript, and Nana did not fail to keep his word.

Meticulously attentive to detail, and fully committed to the project, he demonstrated a desire to achieve absolute perfection, and he put his heart into the autobiography from the moment the French script was translated into English. Displaying an immense talent, he dove right in and crisscrossed every detail in the editorial process as he worked with me to tackle each missing puzzle in the enduring process. He even helped design the book's layout in accordance with my husband's wishes. Thank you, Nana, from the bottom of my heart.

I would also like to extend my heartfelt gratitude to Mr. Regis Zoula, who helped translate the French version of the manuscript into English. This was a process I supervised and monitored to ensure accuracy in the transmission of nuanced expressions in their purest form to the English language prior to being edited by Mr. Yalley. Regis is a very nice and courteous gentleman who handled himself well throughout the process, always ready to undertake any task assigned to him. He was more than happy to become a proofreader, eagerly reading loudly during our sessions and assisting in pertinent research on many occasions.

A very warm thank-you to Mr. Brove Soto, who enjoys all things related to photography. He was more than delighted to scan and adjust all the pictures for the book.

Thank you to Mrs. Caroline Adjoussou, who after reading some of my husband's writing, shared the words that resonated with him: "Uncle, this is really fascinating!" A huge thanks to Mrs. Karine Diby, who worked on the original translation from French to English, and Dr. Alley Djouka, for his contributions throughout the project.

My deep gratitude to Martha Bullen who recommended to create a new book from "Our Common Faith" chapter, for the reader to understand the purpose of Dr. Ghoulem Berrah Foundation and recognize the importance of the topic.

Last but not least, my infinite gratitude goes to the Almighty for blessing me with a unique and wonderful human being and gracing my life with a dream husband.

Made in the USA
Middletown, DE
13 November 2019